BLESSED
are the crazy

breaking the silence about
mental illness, family, and church

To Linda & Barry,

SARAH GRIFFITH LUND

Sarah Griffith Lund

CHALICE
PRESS
ST. LOUIS, MISSOURI

Bible quotations marked NRSV are from the *New Revised Standard Version Bible,* copyright 1989, Division of Christian Education of the National Council of the Churches of Christ in the United States of America. Used by permission. All rights reserved.

Cover art and design: Shawna Everett

www.ChalicePress.com

Print: 9780827202993

EPUB: 9780827203006   EPDF: 9780827203013

Library of Congress Cataloging-in-Publication Data

Lund, Sarah Griffith, 1977-
Blessed are the crazy : breaking the silence about mental illness, family, and church / by Sarah Griffith Lund.
   p. cm.
   ISBN 978-0-8272-0299-3 (pbk.)
1. Lund, Sarah Griffith, 1977- 2. Mentally ill—United States—Biography. 3. Mentally ill—United States—Family relationships.
4. Mental illness—Religious aspects--Christianity. 5. Church work with the mentally ill—United States. I. Title.
RC464.L86A3 2014
616.89—dc23   2014025529

Contents

Study guides for groups interested in discussing *Blessed Are the Crazy* are available on the book's page on ChalicePress.com.

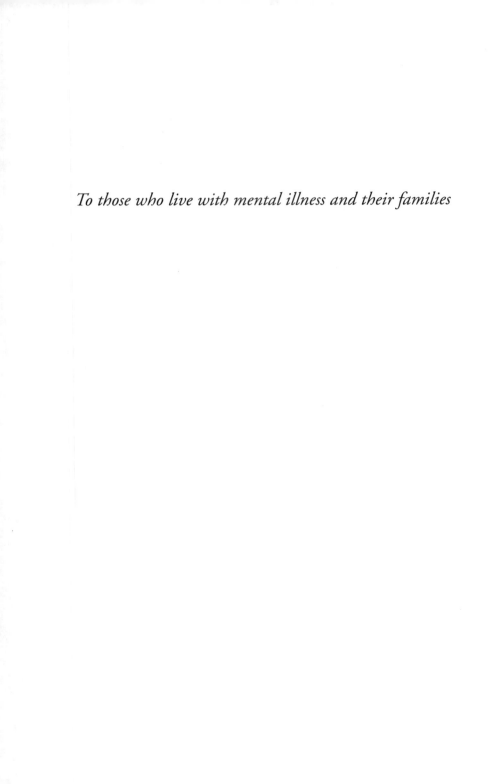

To those who live with mental illness and their families

Definitions

cra * zy (krayzee)

1) a slang word that describes a person with a brain disease

2) a description of a situation that is out of control

cra * zy (krayzee) in the blood (blud)

1) a phrase that describes the genetic predisposition to suffering from a brain disease

   "Bipolar tends to run in families and appears to have a genetic link. Like depression and other serious illnesses, bipolar disorder can also negatively affect spouses, partners, family members, friends and co-workers." (From *BP Magazine,* summer 2014; www.bphope.com.)

2) the reason why some families are more dysfunctional than others

bi * po * lar (bi poler)

1) a brain disease that causes mood swings from the lows of depression to the highs of mania, sometimes referred to as "manic depression"

2) a term that describes having two poles that are extremes

Author's Note

This is my story as I remember it and re-member it. It is a work of non-fiction with a few identifying details changed to protect privacy.

I acknowledge that the language we use to talk about mental illness can be controversial because of various ways it is understood. I use the language that most closely reflects my experiences.

Foreword

It is a real privilege for me to write this foreword, especially as I know that there are others who, by virtue of their personal relationship to Sarah Griffith Lund and/or the role their writings have played in her own healing process, are far more qualified than I to write it.

As you will discover, Sarah has been deeply acquainted with mental illness since her early childhood. One might say that mental illness has been her constant companion, a companion one surely does not seek out or extend a welcoming hand. As she relates in her testimony, her father was mentally ill, her brother is mentally ill, her cousin was executed for a crime that revealed his own mental illness, and she herself has experienced "spiritual visions" that others might consider signs of mental illness.

And yet, hers is an inspiring testimony that reveals the healing powers of the very act of testifying to the brokenness that one has both witnessed and experienced vicariously. As she points out, "The power of our testimonies is the power to work through, heal, and eventually transform our suffering. Telling the stories about my crazy father, bipolar brother, executed cousin, and my own spiritual visions makes room for light and air, the things of God's Spirit, to enter in." Not to have testified as she has done here would have been the real tragedy, more tragic than the mental illnesses recounted in these pages. For, as she also notes, "Keeping these stories as secrets buried deep down in my soul gives them power to hold me captive, isolated by my own fear, shame, and pain: fear that I too, will be labeled crazy and, therefore, unlovable: shame that I am not good enough to be loved; pain because this suffering makes me feel alone in the world."

For the past couple of decades, I have regularly taught a course on the minister and mental illness at Princeton Theological Seminary. This is where Sarah was a student, and, as she testifies, she was there at a time when her cousin Paul was executed for a crime he would not have committed had he been in his "right mind." Because I encourage students to write their papers on the experiences that attracted them to the course in the first place, I have read many papers that, collectively, have taught me that many of our students have experienced the travails of mental illness in their lives, either because they themselves have a mental illness or because a family member or close friend does. Because I taught a course on shame several years prior to teaching the course on mental illness, I have also become aware of the fact that the theologies that have been promoted at the Seminary are overly biased toward guilt and neglectful of the role that shame plays in our sense of wrongness within ourselves and in our relations with others and with God.[1] I learned from students that the first step in the healing process is often the ability to overcome the need of our idealized self to critique—even condemn—our shameful self and to recognize, instead, that God identifies with our shameful self.

Given these experiences with students, I wholeheartedly agree with Sarah's view, presented so eloquently here, that the fundamental key to the process of healing is to *testify* to the role that mental illness has played in our lives and thereby free ourselves from our prisons of fear, shame, and pain, and open the doors to liberated lives based on hope, healing, and love.

Sarah also perceives that we live in a new age as far as mental illness is concerned. She writes, "As a society we are just now beginning to tell our stories in public about mental illness," and that "getting it out in the open—talking about it on the radio, television, in books, on blogs, in schools, and in churches—is progress." For too long the churches have conspired against the telling of these stories. Traditionally, they have done very little to support the mentally ill and their families. However, this is not the time to condemn, but rather to seize the initiative and to encourage the church's leaders to take fuller advantage of the trust that laity invest in them and of the prerogative that comes with being pastors. As I wrote in another foreword, this time for a book by Stewart D. Govig, whose son was diagnosed with schizophrenia in his early twenties:

> Pastors may begin with a ministry of simple *presence*. From this basis, they may proceed to monitor their own—and others'—stigmatizing language. They may *educate* and do so, rather surprisingly, through curricula that is not trendy but traditional, beginning with biblical stories of Jesus' own affinity with the mentally ill. They may also become *advocates*, as Govig himself has become, discovering that the support of a local pastor makes a potent difference among the afflicted families and the wider community. Not least of all, they may become the *receivers*, as have grieving family members, of the witness the mentally ill themselves have to give to the strong who are lost in their own illusions of security. Did not Jesus preach about the man who gathered his grain into barns and assured himself that he had ample goods laid up for many years, only to discover that the things he had prepared were suddenly swept away, in the twinkling of an eye? The mentally ill testify to the folly of such complacency.[2]

For me, the most inspiring story that Sarah tells here is her account of her relationship with her brother Scott, who, like Govig's son John, began to exhibit psychotic behaviors in his senior year in high school. The power of her testimony here is, to me, the fact that her roles as pastor and sibling are interactive and mutually supportive. This is also the case with Govig and his son John. But, as I have noted, pastors are also *receivers* of what the mentally ill have to give to those who consider themselves normal, and Govig expresses this truth when he notes that "John is our teacher."[3] Also compelling to me are the associations that Sarah makes between her brother Scott and Jesus and her suggestion that Jesus had personal knowledge of what it means to be susceptible to mental illness.[4]

Finally, I would like to make a claim for what Sarah has achieved so beautifully here that she—in her modesty—does not claim herself. This is the fact that testimonies like hers play a vitally important role in the *prevention* of mental illness. Her account of her father's irascible behavior and of its particular effects on her brother Scott point to the presence of some "crazy in the blood" in the family that gets passed down from generation to generation. On the other hand, this very testimony tells us that we need not adopt a fatalistic attitude toward mental illness, as if Scott was destined to become mentally ill and there was nothing that could have been done to change this destiny. We are witnessing a new day in the struggle against mental illness, one in which mental health professionals are making significant progress in the area of prevention by identifying persons—typically in their teenage years—who are at risk of serious mental illness (e.g., schizophrenia and bipolar disorder).[5] My prayer is that Sarah's book will fall into the hands of those, including the potentially mentally ill themselves, who will be able to change the predictable future, leaving the "crazy in the blood" behind.

As noted earlier, Sarah confesses that sharing her testimony has set her free from her own prison of fear, shame, and pain. I see her, therefore, as exemplifying the truth that the poet William Stafford expresses in his poem "A Message from the Wanderer": "...Prisoners, listen; / you have relatives outside. And there are / thousands of ways to escape."[6] In this poem, as the Wanderer now sees it, the problem had been that for years he colluded against himself by having chains smuggled to him in pies, or by shouting his plans for escape to the jailers. And yet, all through these years of confinement, "freedom always came nibbling my thought," and at last he noticed that the door was open and no one was there to stop him. As Sarah relates, this was not how it was for her cousin Paul, who was executed at the age of thirty after spending ten years on Death Row. For her, however, it has been different, and all because she has exercised her right—and her gift—to testify to what she has experienced, thus making room for light and air, and for the things of God's Spirit to enter in and enable her to venture forth.

Donald Capps
William Harte Felmeth Professor of
Pastoral Theology (Emeritus) and Adjunct Professor
Princeton Theological Seminary

Preface

In the sweltering end-of-summer heat of 2007, a couple dozen of us show up at the first-ever national gathering for The Young Clergy Women Project. For our time together we have a spirit-guide, a wise sister who is a few steps ahead of us on the journey. Anna Carter Florence speaks to us about the silenced legacy of women whose spirits didn't allow them to remain quiet about the amazing things God was up to in their lives. Despite being told to shut up, pretty up, or leave town, these women preachers blazed a trail into the earth that we are just now uncovering from decades of patriarchy. So, young female preachers are not doing a new thing, even though it is new to some. We are inheritors of an ancient craft, of tales spun by sisters long ago, woven into the fabric of ancient sacred communities. I take comfort in this circle of sisters because we do not need words to explain to one another why it is so good just to be in each other's presence.

Anna tells us that we are living testimonies, whether we like it or not, whether we know it or not. She encourages us to embrace this calling as observers and speakers of truth, and to claim our right to tell our stories in our own voices. We can preach our own testimonies. We can tell our own truths. God gives us permission and the church needs to hear it. We don't have to pretend that everything is okay, because it is not. By the end of the night we are empowered to unearth that God-story embedded within so that we can faithfully share our testimonies. It is in the offering and receiving of testimony that hope can be found. This is what we are born to do.

This is my testimony.

By the time you're done reading my testimony, I hope you will have formed some ideas about how to share your own. Nearly every contour of my life and faith journey has been weathered and shaped by mental illness in my family. In these chapters I unfold my story and discover the surprising ways that God shows up: in a mentally ill father's love, in a suicidal brother's cry for help, in a cousin's dying eyes, and in my own discovery of God's power to heal. It is in the telling of this story that I've come to appreciate how God's blessing is meant for all of us, especially for people who are marginalized and suffering, including those of us with crazy in the blood.

In the conversations with friends, family members, pastors, mentors, spiritual advisors and mental health counselors, I have come to learn that my story is part of the greater story of millions of people whose loved ones suffer from mental illness. Over and over again, in the midst of suffering, God's love has caught me by surprise. I hope that readers of my testimony will encounter surprises too, perhaps in the unexpected ways our stories overlap. I wish it were not so, but chances are good that you (or a loved one) know all too well about the "crazy in the blood" of which I speak.

This testimony is for anybody who has ever wondered how God can use craziness to teach us about the depths of human and divine love. This testimony is for anyone who is afraid to admit that there is a problem with the stigma and shame surrounding mental illness in our churches and in our society, because then the next question is even more foreboding: What can be done about it? This testimony is for you with no faith and you with little faith, and you who run all the committees at your house of worship. And this testimony is even for those of you who are blessed to be free from any crazy in the family blood. This is for you who are both crazy and blessed. Thank you for taking the time to read my testimony. If you haven't already, I encourage you to begin telling your story, too. Write it down, blog it out, tweet it, poetry slam it, sing it, paint it, preach it, and share it. My prayer is that sharing our testimonies sheds some light on a path toward healing and greater peace.

Chapter 1

Learning to Testify

I am five years old. Sometimes my dad is scary. He likes everything to be lots: lots of eating, lots of adventures, lots of sleep, lots of work, lots of yelling, lots of beating, lots of laughing. But he doesn't like lots of me. I don't see him lots. Mommy says he sleeps at the animal hospital now so I snuggle up with her in the California king bed and we cuddle because I am the baby. I am number five. We are Susan, Scott, Steve, Stuart, and Sarah.

It is Sunday morning now. We are in church. My shoes are black. I swing them, tapping the wood with my toes. The singing stops and Mommy holds my hand and says, "It's time to go up." My family stands in line like getting ready for recess, but we don't play in church. Dad says church is for praying, not playing. The minister gives the big people snacks, but this is not snack time because I don't get any. The wafers and wine are not for kids. They are parts of God's body. When it is my turn I put my knees on the pillow and cross my arms over my heart. The minister's big hand covers my head and he leans over me whispering, "May God bless you in the name of the Father, the Son, and the Holy Spirit." My head feels warm. I don't look up. I look down at my dress and count the hearts on it but some are half hearts at the edges. Do the broken hearts count?

My brothers are next to me at the altar and the older two boys are breaking the rules by being rude, making farting sounds and laughing. I didn't fart. We hurry back to sit down. More singing but Dad is not happy. He is crying. Mommy holds my hand. And when the song is over we pray and go home.

Sometimes after church we get fancy pie but not today. Dad is driving the car fast past the pie place. My brothers cry out for pie. Dad says we were bad in church, so no pie for bad children. But I wasn't bad. My brothers cry out, "We want pie!" And the car stops. Dad gets out of the car and pulls off his belt. He opens the car door and grabs my oldest two brothers. They scream with their pants down and their underwear touches their shoes. He whips them and the other cars on the road drive by fast. They get back into the car. This time Mommy is crying. I wish the hearts on my dress were stickers; then I would use them for band-aids.

It is night time. But Dad needs help at the animal hospital and we all want to go. On the way there we get snacks at the drive-thru. We get lots of paper bags with twenty hamburgers and French fries. Dad is hungry tonight and needs energy for work. There are two dogs scheduled for surgeries so my brothers and sister help my dad in the operation room. Being the baby means that I am too little to do the surgeries. I go down the hall to the room with the cages where all the cats and dogs sleep. I crawl into an empty bottom cage and pretend I am a cat. Today I don't have to clean the stinky cages and throw away the pee pee newspaper.

Only the dogs are getting surgeries now, not me or my brothers or sister. If we get sick or hurt we go to the animal hospital and get dog shots because we are the same size as dogs. Just the other day when I cut my head open jumping on the bed, Dad said to wrap it in a wet towel to stop the bleeding. Mommy wanted to call the doctor but Dad said no. Now we know that whenever there is blood to get into the shower. My head stopped bleeding, but you can still feel a dent. I close the wire door and stay inside the cage until it's time to go home.

Home Is Where God Is?

Home is where God is, but God wasn't always living with us at 1908 Angola Avenue in California. *If God is love,* my ten-year-old mind reasoned, *then how could God live in a house where there is such hate?* I wondered that when my dad and my oldest brother, Scott, were having one of their fights. This time it got so bad that Dad chased him out of the house. I followed them, wanting to see for myself what happened next. Would this be the time that my dad killed my brother or would it be the other way around? This time Dad confiscated my brother's prized skateboard and started to drive off in the truck, probably going to throw it in the city dump. Just then my brother ran up to the truck door and hurled his thin body through the open window, practically climbing into my dad's lap to get his skateboard back. But when my brother leaned in, the truck suddenly reversed and my brother smacked to the ground, screaming, the truck tires screeching as my dad drove off down the street. While my brother lay there writhing in pain with a fractured leg, I saw the look of betrayal and abandonment on his bloody face. Dark streams of blood stained his dirty blond mohawk. God gave us the most horrible, twisted, and awful father who ever lived. Without a doubt he hated us all and he was going to kill us.

Soon after the hit-and-run, Mom dragged us all to family counseling to figure out what to do. She wanted to know if she could save her marriage and keep the family safe from our father's rages. The counselor stared at us through thick black-framed glasses and then asked us kids to vote. He said to raise our hands up high if we wanted to split the family up and leave our father behind in his own miserable mess. In the dimly lit room I was unsettled. This man who looked so serious—did he really not know what we should do? I shrank in the darkness of the unknown. I couldn't move my hand, let alone think about moving my whole life.

What I did know was that my stomach hurt, bad. In it was a feeling that something was irreversibly wrong, hitched to a sense of an impending domestic nuclear disaster. After the counseling appointment we went home and packed black trash bags with underwear, shoes, shirts, and shorts. Into superhero and Strawberry Shortcake pillowcases we stuffed pieces of our childhood: handmade baby blankets, baby books, and home

videos of births. The Christmas ornaments given to me by my
godparents, several from each of my ten years, were considered
unessential. We crammed all this into the blue and white
Suburban, along with our bodies—five kids and a mom—plus
the roll top desk and grandfather clock. Mom couldn't bear to
part with those.

That summer, in the middle of the night, with pregnant
avocados hanging heavy on the tree branches, we left Angola,
moving out in secret, without saying a word to any of our friends.
We moved to Missouri to live with my mom's parents. If God
is good, then God was glad that we were finally gone from that
house where hate scared love away.

Moving to Missouri put geographic distance between me
and my father, but the fear of him remained smack dab in the
middle of my heart. He figured out right away what we had
done and he tracked us down, making harassing phone calls to
my grandparents' house where we stayed. He threatened their
lives too, blaming them for stealing his children. My mother
warned me to never go with my father anywhere if he showed
up to take me, and to never let him into the house. In addition
to my chronic stomach pain I started wetting the bed. With
my dolls I made up imaginary worlds. We needed to go to the
doctor, but didn't. No money. But still…nothing was so bad
now, was it? We were all still alive.

My father remained in California while we made Missouri
our new home. In California we had lived in a ranch house,
had a live-in nanny, gardeners, and a pony. In Missouri, Mom
worked as a public school teacher, but Dad didn't pay child
support. Mom explained that he wasn't being lazy; he couldn't
work because of his disability. Whatever that was—no one
would tell us exactly. When we weren't in school, all five of us
kids worked: paper routes, washing dishes, waitressing, tutoring,
and babysitting. But we were still poor. Food stamps, free lunch
programs at school, and secondhand clothes were all new to me.
I repeatedly had to tell the cashier in the lunchroom, in front of
my friends, that I was "free lunch." I decided to bring my lunch

to school and nobody needed to know it was paid for with food stamps. I could at least try to pretend I wasn't poor.

How He Loved Us

That same year Dad managed to trick my mom and "abduct" my middle brother Steve for part of the junior high school year. At first Dad had both Steve and Stuart with him for a short visit during the summer, but Dad then decided to send Stuart home and keep Steve. Mom remembers picking Stuart up at the airport, shocked to find him by himself. She says that Stuart was so traumatized by his older brother Steve's abduction (in part wondering why Dad hadn't wanted him as well) that he was temporarily mute, in addition to his chronic stutter, and couldn't tell Mom why Steve wasn't with him or why he was sent back home on the airplane by himself.

Steve was just starting junior high and he remembers living with Dad in a God-forsaken part of Los Angeles, eating strictly a fast-food diet of fried chicken, burgers, milkshakes, and French fries. The small hotel room was crammed with piles of magazines, stacks of boxes, and old fast-food wrappers carpeting the floor. It was fun for Steve for a while, a new adventure, but it sort of got old and none of his friends were at his new school. I talked to Steve on the phone a few times when his allergies were bad. He sounded really stuffed up; maybe he wasn't getting to the doctor. After a few months, my dad grew tired of my brother and sent him back to Missouri on an airplane with tickets purchased by my grandparents.

In my father's world, he was a man of global political importance. He was distressed at being targeted and followed by undercover spies because he harbored secret information about a plot to kill the Queen of England. He knew he would be famous some day for his inventions, like underground tunnels connecting continents. He became totally brainwashed by Lyndon LaRouche, a political figure whose movement attracted followers with its claims to have secret, inside information about United States history and government. They boasted about ownership of privileged information about communist plots, assassination attempts, and scandalous connections to British aristocracy, as well as the hidden influences of Thomas Jefferson on modern politics. Instead of trying to repair our family, he joined LaRouche's new family.

He was furious that we left him. He accused Mom of being a lesbian. He'd call to enlighten us about LaRouche. At first I sincerely tried to listen and understand what it was all about, but it got too weird. AIDS, he told us, was invented as a Soviet war machine. Harvard University is a center for fascism. The Episcopal Church is the assassination arm of British intelligence. *Really?*

I knew Dad was smart. He married my mom. I knew he had important ideas. He owned one of the first emergency animal hospitals in the city. But what I really didn't know until later was that he was also sick. He covered up his mental illness so well, hiding it behind his intelligence, work ethic, charisma, and love for life. It was hard to tell sometimes whether he was manic or just excited about a new project. But as he got older, and we kids grew older, his mental illness remained untreated, and his symptoms grew more pronounced. It wasn't until we moved to Missouri that I realized there was something wrong with the way Dad's brain worked. He had a zig-zag way of telling us things. There was always another version of the truth, a secret story that only he knew.

My father mailed us boxes of "educational literature" from the LaRouche organization. We leafed through the pages, laughing in disbelief and concealed grief. In a way, the boxes were like care packages. I guess this propaganda was his love language, his way of communicating how much he cared about us. Where he had once insisted that we go to church, he had now adopted LaRouche as his religion, and now the salvation of his family was at stake. It was his job to save us. We didn't throw out the boxes; we just stacked them in our basement family room right next to the Nintendo game station. My father's slanted handwriting in black ink on the brown cardboard lid linked me to him. Inside those boxes there was some trace of my father's love.

When he called the house I usually got stuck on the phone with him the longest because my brothers and sister refused to talk with him or only listened briefly and then handed the phone over to me. With one ear I would listen to him ranting manically nonstop about LaRouche while the other ear was trying to follow *The Cosby Show* on TV. The part of me that listened to him felt flattered to be the chosen one, and strangely loved by his attention, even if it was garbled nonsense. Somehow I was important to my father. Maybe there was a part of him that wasn't crazy and could still love me? Maybe it was all a big mistake, a misunderstanding? He could get better if he wanted to, and, if he loved us enough, he would.

No One Asked

I even prayed about it, asking God to help me understand why love had to be so confusing and painful. Sunday mornings I ran down the street to church and headed straight to the donut table in the fellowship hall. The ministers and kind strangers at our church helped me know that not everything in my life was ruined. At ten, I liked going to church and hearing about my Father God and his love. It made my stomach not hurt so bad, despite my filling it with donuts.

Church taught me a lot about a loving God, but not how to tell my own story about love, or the lack of it. My Sunday school teachers wanted me to learn about God's love for the world and that this love sent Jesus to save us. But no one in Sunday school ever asked me what I needed saving from in my own life. Bible truths would magically set us free from sin. Yet there was no place for us to name, in our own words, the sin in our lives, the sinfulness of our families, or the sinfulness of our world.

None of my closest friends knew my father was crazy. I buried all my feelings of abandonment, neglect, rejection, anger, and fear deep down inside. I spent time with my friends and their dads, the ones who coached my soccer team or drove me and my friends around after school; dads who were at home to eat family dinners. I spent lots of time at my best friend Jill's house. She seemed to have the perfect life: only one brother, a mom, and a dad.

It's seventh grade math class and I'm sitting at my desk in the back of the classroom trying to figure out the surface area of a cylinder. Someone comes into the classroom and hands the math teacher a note. The teacher calls my name and my heart races as I walk up front in-between the narrow rows of desks, embarrassed that my shorts are sticking to the back of my thighs. The freaky boy in the front row is looking at my big butt. The teacher hands me the note. It is yellow office paper and it says, "Sarah Griffith. Come to office. Father is here for early pick up."

My mother is dead.

Why else would my father come all they way to Missouri from California to get me? That would be the only reason he would come. Confused and terrified I quickly walk back to my desk to get my pink Guess book bag. Running down the hallway and up the stairs to the school office, I fear for my life. What is going on? Where is my mom? Then I see him and my stomach knots. He's waiting for me, sitting on the white plastic office chair. "Come on," he says standing up, "let's go." I look to the school administrator, wondering if she thinks it is safe to go with him, and she smiles, nodding. She doesn't know anything about my father. I do not say a word, but follow him out to the parking lot where we get into his rusted-out old truck. "So, where do you want to go? I thought we could get a bite to eat," he says. He is oblivious to how scary and infuriating this is for me.

"Does Mom know you are here?" I ask. "No," he says. I haven't seen him for three years. He thinks he can take me out of school, and then try to buy my love with food. "Take me home now. I have to do my paper route," I blurt out. "Oh, come on. Aren't you hungry?" He laughs. "Let me get you something," he argues. "I want to go home," I repeat as I roll down the truck window. The clouds briefly cover the sun and a bird cries out.

He starts the truck and we putter out of the school parking lot. Across the street the dogwood trees are in bloom, and their white petals are traced with pink. I direct him how to get home.

Thoughts race through my mind: What does he want with me? What if he doesn't take me home? Even with the window down, I'm suffocating, trapped inside the truck with him. It smells like stale French fries. He drives slowly past our church before turning down the street to my house. My stomach turns somersaults.

The truck engine dies in front of my house on Highland Drive. The grass is too long and looks white trash; the gray house paint is peeling. "Thanks for the ride home," I mutter while reaching for the truck door. His giant hand grabs my arm. "Stay with me," he pleads. I pull my arm away from him and pause for a moment. I close my eyes and feel safety in the sunshine streaming down on me from above. Nothing bad can happen to me in the daylight. Now that I'm home, I'm almost free. He can't hurt me here. He wouldn't dare.

A green van pulls up into the driveway, and a guy unloads five bundles of newspapers, and piles them by the steps, one on top of another, before driving away. "Well, I've got to go do my paper route." I open the truck door, grab my book bag, and get out. Closing the door I take a hard look at him. I don't know who he is, really, or what he is capable of doing to me. I turn away. Walking up to the house I see the school bus coming and it stops at the tall oak tree. And there, in his dilapidated truck, my dad drives away, following the yellow school bus down the road.

Someone's Girlfriend, Someone Else's Story

Even though I have three older brothers, unless we were fighting over what food remained in the house, we pretty much ignored each other. The only boys I paid any real attention to were the ones who liked me. In junior high I discovered that boys gave me some of the attention and affection I craved, even if it wasn't real love. Chasing and being chased by boys was a marvelous distraction from dealing with my father. It was nothing to sneak out of the house late at night and return in the early morning, undetected, in time for church. Sexual relationships with boys made me feel important and alive—

powerful, even. But by the end of high school that wasn't new anymore, and the power behind it faded. Something was still missing. I longed to be more than somebody's girlfriend, so-and-so's little sister, or a crazy man's daughter.

In high school I wrote for the school newspaper. I loved seeking out and telling other people's stories, uncovering their hidden strengths—such as the star tennis athlete's success despite severe scoliosis. I also looked for ways to challenge injustices such as homophobia. Focusing on other people's stories allowed me to forget about my own for awhile. This was my first experience with testimony as I wove together stories of other people's truths.

My energy suddenly shifted after injuring my foot during tryouts for the high school girls soccer team. I'd always played sports. I felt strong. I felt like I mattered. But now, at age sixteen, although I made the high school soccer team, with a broken toe I couldn't play. So instead of throwing myself into athletic training, I left my body and entered my head. I began writing poems and taking photographs, publishing them in the high school literary magazine. It was an awkward metamorphosis, from girl jock to artsy-angst girl. One poem was about how lonely I was after my best friend and I broke up over a boy, and some of the photographs were of her before our friendship ended. The magazine also published photos from one of my trips to the local car junkyard, with images showcasing the mechanical and metallic details of brokenness and abandonment. These inanimate objects gave testimony to how I felt…thrown away and forgotten.

Starting to Tell My Story

During my senior year of high school I signed up for a two-hour Advanced Placement art class. In a way that Sunday school couldn't, creating art helped me begin to tell my own story. Through layers of colors, shapes, and textures, I expressed what was going on inside my mind and heart. Mixing media—markers, acrylics, pencils—and making my own geometric stamps out of cardboard, I layered colors, shapes, and images. First yellow triangles, then red circles, followed by purple rectangles, all one on top of another, blurring boundaries and shapes. Something inside of me broke open in art and spilled out onto paper.

I remember that as I painted, I spoke to none of the other students in the class, wanting to totally disappear into the changing colors. I simply moved my body, hands and eyes, connecting paint to paper without thinking. In the art, I created my own reality, free from other people's definitions or expectations. I made my own sanctuary in the swirling colors of paint. When the paint dried, I crammed the paintings into my thickening portfolio. I didn't look at them again until the end of the year, when I laid out all the pieces, and they covered the entire surface of all the tables in the class room. It looked like a rainbow exploded. Something I could not articulate in words found fluency in art. My art teacher nominated me as "most improved student" at the senior class awards ceremony. I was shocked. It was the first time I realized that telling my story through art allowed me to express my true self and also connected me to others.

Burying God

I am eighteen years old and a member of the 1995 senior class at David H. Hickman High School, home of the bare-bottom Kewpie baby doll mascot. It's my last summer before starting college in San Antonio and, thanks to Mom's credit card, I'm touring England, Wales, and Scotland with my family in a rented minivan. Following a tasty seaside fish and chips lunch, we've wandered off on our separate ways. Now I am alone, sitting on top of an ancient stone wall that hugs the British seashore. I imagine the wall was built by fathers, sons, and brothers long ago. Looking out, the dark blue-gray waters reflect a calm unknown in my soul, eerily blurring water and sky. The sharp, cold air penetrates my exposed round face and I stuff my naked hands down into my pockets.

For a moment my identity is so entirely separate from the earth, water, wind, and sky (there is no sun) that I feel alien and alone. Is this my planet? Is this my home? What if there is no home for me anywhere? This is the truth that I feel within my bones. Could it be that there is no God and there is no love, as I had hoped for all of this time? I am a fool.

Where does my hope come from?

It doesn't come. My hope is far away, lost at sea. Desperate, my spirit dives into the sea in search of hope. I wait…but nothing. My hope and my spirit have drowned together, like a rescue mission gone horribly wrong.

I give up. Putting my black knock-off Doc Martin shoes back down onto the pebbled earth, I turn away from the vast sea with fresh conviction: God has stopped breathing and I have buried him deep below.

Hope from the Crypt

Even though I buried God in the North Sea, I ended up going to seminary. The story of how an atheist teenager sitting on a stone seawall became a young clergy woman praying in a cold crypt is a testimony you will soon hear. But first, this is what you need to know: my dad is buried too.

I buried my father in the hilltop family cemetery that pokes up out of the fertile Missouri farmland. Under the earth my father's cremains rest inside a sky-blue papier-mâché box that I ordered via the Internet. The box was advertised to disintegrate over time, leaving no carbon, size 14, extra-wide footprint behind. His massive six foot two, 300-plus pound body, ground down to fit into a shoe box, was still a little heavy, but now weighed no more than an old-fashioned family Bible. I wonder if parts of him were mistakenly left behind in the incinerator or mixed in with someone else. It wouldn't be the first time he wasn't all there.

Instead of staying with family in Missouri, or flying back home to Florida with my newly wedded husband, I choose to go to Washington, D.C., for solace, healing, and affirmation. It is the first-ever national gathering for The Young Clergy Women Project. I need to be here, alone with familiar strangers, so that

I can look into my soul's mirror and see it anew with God's eyes. I'm thousands of miles away from my dead father, but standing here in the National Cathedral crypt, wearing flip-flops, jeans, and a T-shirt, I finally feel his death. The crypt, a womblike space carved out of the earth, holds my exhausted body, salty tears, heavy sighs, and in the quiet I realize just what a wreck I really am. I am here, but just barely.

My thoughts are interrupted by the lightness of my sisters' cheerful laughter and a parade of footsteps echoing through the cold stone corridors. Opening worship begins in a few minutes. I welcome them into the crypt chapel with a faint smile, not even trying to put on a fake face. This is a place where I can be real with no apologies. I am dead tired. I'm not the one in charge and I don't need to make sure everyone else is okay. For once during worship I have the freedom to pay attention to my own spirit, to listen to my inward voice and to feel the emotions that are just too big to stay inside anymore.

Perhaps I am not the only one who feels this way. There are others who come and sit near me and they too look alone in their thoughts. Gathering here, we all come from different places, but we carry a similar heaviness. We're misunderstood and out-of-place in a beloved church that often views our very existence as foreign and as an obstacle to overcome. We are God's chosen leaders faithfully doing our work, but too many times we do it without the support and encouragement of kindred spirits. So that is why we are physically here together in this space, for such a time as this.

We come from marriages (often fragile and new), from resigned singleness, from the raw nipples of first-time motherhood, from rural churches, from urban churches, from hospitals and universities, from messed-up places, and from surprisingly healthy places. We come from Anglican, Lutheran, Baptist, Methodist, Episcopal, Presbyterian, Reformed, Congregational, and Christian traditions. We come. And that's what really counts—the fact that by some act of God's grace, we are all here tonight in this cathedral crypt. And we are singing and we are crying, and we are laughing, and we are dancing with our shoes off. We want to feel the ground beneath our feet; we want to know what it is that holds us up.

We are here because we want to do ministry without dying—dying to our true selves, dying from loneliness, dying from suffocation. And tonight, in this place of death, we are pregnant with hope.

chapter 2

Entrusting My Father to God's Beloved Community

Along with quitting God that summer, I quit shaving my legs. I figured that since I felt unlovable, I might as well feel untouchable too. Hairy legs became the Do Not Enter sign on my body. My self-esteem was at an all time low, while my waistline was at an all time high. I hid inside of plus-size baggy pants and loose fitting shirts. By the time I drove a thousand miles to college, I was ready for my life to be over and, in its place, something new to be born. I was over feeling gutted out and empty, disconnected and alone. I hungered for new friends like a neglected dog waiting for bread crumbs to fall from the table.

Then the first day on campus I met a Jesus freak. I first heard Naomi's voice, bright and soulful, echoing down the hallway into my dorm room. I peeked into the room and saw a brown-skinned girl strumming a guitar, with long, thick, dark-chocolate hair fanning across her back. She looked up and smiled. In her eyes I saw that she was hoping to start over too. Quickly I learned three important things about Naomi: she grew up just miles away from campus, she was a Pakistani American, and she loved Jesus. All of this intrigued me, except for the Jesus part. That was weird and kind of scary. She seemed obsessed or was she possessed?

I soon found out she didn't just love Jesus, but she was crazy about him and worshiped him. Yet she seemed so intelligent. The journalist inside of me was hooked and wanted to know her whole story. How could this beautiful, talented, international, smart young woman talk about Jesus like he was sitting on the bed right next to her, holding her hand? It turns out she was raised a Southern Baptist, and in the South no one takes Jesus lightly. Jesus was the King, and the King is in the building. Naomi and I got to know each other, bonding during late night gooey chocolate chip cookie binges, so I figured I could ignore the Jesus part.

In between cookie gorging, classes, and sleep, we began regularly attending small group Bible studies held in other students' dorm rooms. We sat in circles on grubby dorm room floors, holding open Bibles, all of us lost and shy souls, desperate for alternatives to the all-you-can-eat buffet of parties, beer, and hazing. I will always be grateful for the student leaders of the InterVarsity Christian Fellowship, an on-campus ministry, who did everything possible to make Christianity attractive to college students. Their best strategy for attracting new students was to host free events on campus that offered all-you-could-eat pizza and all-you-could-stand friendship during a fragile time in my life. It was also the first time I had ever experienced contemporary worship or sung a praise song with people who used their bodies expressively in worship: hand clapping, raising their arms above their heads, and jumping up and down. Their behavior and the sincere place it seemed to come from baffled me. Even though I hung out with born-again Christians, I remained skeptical of the power of faith in my own life, and was pretty sure that God was right where I left him, buried underneath the North Sea.

My freshman classes opened my eyes to theories about family systems, human psychology, and feminist ideology. It didn't take long before this new information put my personal family experience in a different perspective. I began to rethink my old classifications of my father, and to realize that much of his abusive behavior resulted from untreated bipolar disorder. Learning about mental illness helped me to not blame myself for his neglect. For the first time, I started to feel some compassion towards him, understanding that he was suffering too. What became difficult was that, even though my feelings towards my father changed, our relationship remained strained. As time went on and my father's untreated mental illness progressively got worse, I didn't hear from him as much. I began to fear that he might be dead. I imagined that he would die homeless and alone somewhere and I would never know. I felt sorry for myself, thinking that not only was God the Father lost to me forever, but my birth father was lost too.

Part of the tragedy about my father's life was that he was missing out on so many proud, special moments in our family of five kids: graduations from colleges, graduate school, and medical school; weddings; and births. He was missing out on little things too: soccer games, pizza nights, and band concerts. I began to want to see him for the first time in a very long time. He was no longer a bad person; he was a person who suffered from an untreated brain disease. But, more than that, he was my father, not just some crazy person.

I couldn't help noticing that I'd begun considering my father from a perspective of Christian mercy. The nights of Bible study, my dear friend's Jesus talk, and the sincere faith of other students began to help me see that maybe I actually did hope to believe in God, after all. And not only believe in the existence of God, but believe that God knows me, loves me, and desires to be in an intimate relationship with me. Countless nights of Bible study ended with students praying fervently for my salvation. But there is *hoping to believe,* and then there is *taking the plunge*: diving head first right down into that cold, wild North sea, rolling the stone away from the tomb, and resurrecting God for yourself.

Freed to Forgive

A few weeks later, I attended a retreat organized by our Christian campus ministry. Underneath the open sky in the rugged wilderness of the Texas hill country, I said an evangelical version of the Jesus prayer: "Lord Jesus Christ, son of God, have mercy on me, a sinner." Crying out to God for help, cradled in Naomi's arms, I asked God for forgiveness and mercy. During this time of prayer I emptied my heart and mind of all the anger, resentment, bitterness, and fear that I carried with me to college. Viewed through the lens of faith, these were the things that kept me apart from God and unable to accept love. I had been preoccupied with my own suffering. Asking Jesus to save me meant being healed from all that harmed my mind and spirit.

I asked my Father God to totally fill that void in my life. Growing up in the church, I knew about God; the Bible stories of creation, floods, lions, lambs, multiplying loaves of bread; and baby Jesus. But this was the first time I acknowledged that I needed God to do something really important for me. I asked God to take away the anger and fear I had carried for a thousand miles. I asked for forgiveness. And in return I knew that I could begin to forgive my father. I wanted to forgive my father. Even though I still felt the pain that his illness caused, I no longer took it personally. I no longer resented him for having a mental illness. I could let go and be free.

What remains with me about that specific encounter with God is the memory of total surrender and union, the consummation of my soul. And I remember being baptized by the wet and sticky uncontrollable tears and snot that gushed out of my body and spilled onto the dry earth.

My body was weak, so with Naomi's help I got up off the dusty ground. The retreat had produced a new convert. With the evangelical brand of Christianity freshly stamped on my forehead, once back on campus I continued on a course of daily Bible study and prayer. I recall the incredible lightness I felt as I walked to class one morning, realizing that I no longer carried hatred or resentment or anger towards my father. By asking God for forgiveness and receiving the gift of new life in Christ, I was able to let go of these painful parts of my past. I let go of my unmet needs and expectations from my earthly father and, in their place, began to focus on deepening my relationship with my heavenly Father. I desired a closer connection to God. I desired to know God completely, to love God and be loved by God. I actually considered taking a leave of absence from school so I could focus all my energies on God, but my English professor counseled me to stay in college and pursue God along with my other studies. I'm glad I took her wise advice; without the daily rhythms of going to class and meeting up for Bible studies my pursuit of God might have overwhelmed me. I didn't see then how important my community was in providing structure and support in my journey.

I found myself spending time alone in the campus Parker Chapel late afternoons or in the evenings. The doors were always unlocked. A few times I exchanged smiles with the Spanish-speaking custodians quietly keeping God's house in order. One night I lay down on the red carpet in front of the altar. With my arms spread out open and my eyes looking up I stayed there for what seemed to be hours. A peace washed over me and I felt tension leaving my body from head to toes. Years later, in my practice of yoga, a similar feeling of relaxation and peace comes to me as I lie on the mat in meditation, surrendering myself to the universe.

As Easter approached at the end of my freshman year, I found myself thinking about my life in terms of the Christian themes of death and rebirth. Although faithfully baptized in the Lutheran church as an infant, I wanted to mark my spiritual rebirth with baptism by immersion—not because the first one "didn't take" or because I thought I ever carried the seed of Eve's original sin. I wanted a believer's baptism. I wanted to celebrate on Easter Sunday because ever since that day in the hill country under the big Texas sky, I felt like my spirit was born again from above, just like Jesus said. Even though Easter was a week away, being that it was the South, it was easy to find a church willing to squeeze me onto their baptism roster, just like throwing another fish into the fryer. So that Easter morning, dressed in a white cotton robe over my clothes, standing before the worshiping congregation, I entered the baptismal pool with the pastor. And as he lifted my dripping body out of the tepid water, he accidentally whacked my head so hard against the fiberglass pool that it caused a thunderous sound to echo through my ears.

A New View of Beloved Community

My new community of faith affirmed God's power and the fact that I could earnestly ask God for anything, but my need to grow in Christ soon developed beyond what those friends could offer. In that particular faith community, I experienced a narrowness that sparked a new interest in seeking out God for myself, a God free from religious rules and limitations. What scared me the most was that as part of this community I had begun to replace critical thinking with blind faith. When the Bible study leaders said homosexuality and pre-marital sex were sins, I didn't struggle too hard to question those teachings. Looking back, I see these as my weakest moments as a Christian—when I allowed the thinking of others to replace my own.

After a little more than a year with this campus ministry, I grew more and more uncomfortable with the dogmatic theology and moral code that encouraged an unhealthy practice of casting judgment on my gay and sexually active peers. Meanwhile, the courses in my chosen major of religious studies opened my mind to think critically about my newfound faith. They shattered easy assumptions and pushed aside pat answers. What would Jesus think when he saw that Christianity had become just another college sorority?

I began to crave encounters with God off campus. In the cafeteria I saw a flier from the student volunteer organization saying they needed people to spend the night at the inner city homeless shelter. The job was to stay awake and keep watch over the men and women who slept there, and to be company for those who couldn't sleep. At the shelter, we could admit people up until 8 p.m., but we had to keep the door locked afterward. The dorms at the shelter, smelling stale and sweet from a mixture of body odor and baby powder, filled with nearly a hundred sleeping people on cots. In the dead of the night the shelter was surprisingly and mercifully quiet. Then, by six o'clock in the morning all the guests had to be out of the building. As they left, we handed each person a bologna sandwich and Styrofoam cup of hot coffee. We'd match up their baggage claim ticket with any belongings they had asked to have stored in the locked room. A handful of folks had extra early wake-up calls, 3 or 4 a.m., in order to catch a bus to get to work across town. After all the guests left, we drove back to campus to make it in time for the first morning class.

At the homeless shelter I experienced a sense of Christian community that felt unscripted and nonjudgmental. More than that, for the first time I felt a calling to ministry. It was deeply satisfying to offer myself in service to people who needed me. And it was more than that. I felt it was part of my redemption. By spending time at the homeless shelter, I believed that I was spending time with my Father God, offering kindness, compassion, and physical help. I saw the living Christ in the faces of the people I served. I also saw my birth father in the faces of the men who shuffled by, pockets stuffed with crumpled paper, glasses cracked and ill-fitting, shoes stretched out and worn. By now my family was not sure where my father was living; the last we heard he was living out of his truck. I guessed that some of the men in my shelter had daughters that they hadn't been on good terms with for years. Soon I became the coordinator of the shelter's volunteer program and recruited other college students to join me for overnight duty. At the shelter I gave myself as an offering to my Father God, praying that through kindness and compassion, I would be one with God.

I also realize that there were selfish reasons why I worked with people who were homeless. I felt helpless because there wasn't anything I could do about my father's mental illness. I was drawn to work with the homeless (and often times mentally ill) as a way to feel closer to my father. Just as I was volunteering to help them, I knew they were helping me too. Being with the community of God's homeless people helped me form a better understanding of my life. I knew that the homeless people in San Antonio had families too, just like my father far away in Los Angeles. The families who had become estranged from their homeless and mentally ill relatives had valid reasons for doing so. Sometimes as family members we simply cannot be the ones to help them, but we need to trust that others can and will. And there were some compassionate people in L.A. who helped my father.

I never told my father that next to Jesus, he was my greatest spiritual teacher. The inner struggle with what it meant to have a mentally ill father that taught me about the rough edges of forgiveness. It was clear by my senior year of college that I wanted to go to seminary to pursue training for full-time ministry. I chose a program that offered a dual track of divinity studies and social work. For me the gospel went hand in hand with practical humanitarian services. Not only was I to preach the good news, I was to empower people to experience it now in this world. At the heart of Jesus' message is the mandate to feed the hungry, clothe the naked, visit the sick, and take care of the poor. I wanted the education and training to equip me for this kind of ministry. Freedom from abusive relationships, isolation, and depression were important parts of my vision of the kingdom of God. God wants for us to be not a sorority with a Jesus mascot but a Beloved Community, where people come together for justice, peace, and redemptive love. I focused my social work and ministry training on working with survivors of domestic violence. My father's untreated mental illness meant that my mother was a survivor of domestic violence and so was I. In my graduate social work studies I could further reflect on how my own family system (and the mental illness within it) impacted my identity and sense of call to ministry. Again, I found my vocation's satisfaction in the connection I felt with the people I served. I could relate to survivors of domestic violence and I understood the fear and anger that held them prisoner. I also knew that the struggle for freedom was worth the fight.

A Word of God for Outcasts

Not every preacher can say that her first sermon fell on hungover ears. A summer internship during seminary led me to the streets of Glasgow, Scotland, working as a chaplain for the Church of Scotland's inner city day center. Sitting in a metal folding chair in the dining room of the day center, I preached from a manuscript I had carefully crafted by using the exegetical method taught by my erudite seminary professors. Thick Scottish stew simmered in the kitchen while men and women slumped in the congregation, stomachs growling and eyelids drooping. About halfway through the sermon people started getting up and walking outside. But a few smiled, and I wrapped up the three main points. It was a quick lesson for me about context. I didn't have a clue about the people I was serving. But as the weeks went by, I listened to their stories and began to hear what mattered to them. By the end of our time together, I had organized a trip for twelve people to get out of the industrial city and stay at a retreat center on Iona, a remote and holy island off Scotland's west coast. They wanted to get away from the everyday grind of soup kitchens, concrete sidewalks, and cramped living quarters.

In one of our planning meetings the group decided to institute one rule for the trip: everyone had to remain sober. This was going to be hardest for Robert, a young man who regularly participated in Bible study, but then would disappear for days at a time. In childhood he served as an altar boy in the Catholic Church, and now in adulthood he felt he was an embarrassment to his family. It was Robert who didn't show up at the Glasgow train station the morning we departed for Iona. My heart sank. Of all the guys who needed this retreat, I believed he needed it the most. We boarded the train and took our seats, excited and anxious about the day's travel that required multiple modes of transportation: train, bus, ferry, and van ride. About three hours into the train ride, I was shocked to see Robert walking into our train car with a big grin on his face, stinking to high heaven. It turns out that Robert had boarded the train at a different station and was hiding out in the lounge car. We had to decide whether or not he could continue traveling with us, since within the first few hours of the journey to Iona he broke the only rule we had. The guys wanted to give him another chance. When we arrived at Iona, Robert spent the next twenty-four hours in the Iona Guest House sleeping off his hangover.

While on retreat we ate wholesome homemade food, walked the pilgrim's path through the tall grass, and lived inside the walls of sacred and intentional community. Many of the men suffered from mental illness, but that made their retreat to Iona even more meaningful. For the first time, at the Iona Community they were treated not as crazy outcasts but as honored guests, a valuable part of Beloved Community.

My Drop-in Family

After graduation from seminary I was ordained into Christian ministry at the donut church down the street from the house we moved to in Missouri. It was the church that had accepted my broken family, and didn't ask questions about why we were crazy. What mattered most was that it was the community that first nurtured my understanding of a loving God. Following my ordination, I continued in graduate school for another year to complete a degree in social work. During that time I worked as a chaplain for a domestic violence agency in New Jersey. This is where I heard stories firsthand from women about the dangerous power of spiritual abuse; stories about how abusive husbands were a "cross to bear." I also heard stories of courage as women struggled to break free from cycles of abuse, years of domestic torture. As a young women fresh out of grad school, I sometimes wondered how it was that I could be of any help to these women, pouring out their souls to me. Yet, it was the holy task of listening, of hearing, of seeing them that mattered. For women beaten down by words and hands, to speak without fear is redemptive.

Hearing these stories of struggle raised my awareness of the need for a counter-narrative. Where were the stories of hope? For me, that's the transformative power of the Christian faith and the story that the church can share with the world: stories of hope, stories of healing, stories of resurrection. I realized that I wanted my ministry to be grounded in the church. So I accepted a position as an outreach minister at an inner city

Minneapolis church. I felt called to be in congregational ministry because I believe that, as Christians, our worshiping life has the potential to inspire faithful action in the world. From the scripture, prayers, sacraments, and gathered body of Christ on Sunday come every other day's motivation to do justice, seek peace, and love all as Christ loves. I also felt called to preach Jesus' mandate to love God and love our neighbors as ourselves. The church, on its best days, is the community where the power of God's love can transform us from hopeless orphans to faithful children of our Father God.

As I grew closer to God, I thought about my father more and more. By the time I lived in Minneapolis, I knew that my father was still out in California and living with a friend. One night I called him. He was very depressed. The way he talked, it sounded like he was going to kill himself. Frightened for him, when I got off the phone I informed the local police, who went to check on him. Then I called one of my spiritual mentors and asked her to pray for my father. The police called me back and said that he seemed to be in no danger. But I worried. After that he didn't answer my calls. I guessed that he was angry with me for calling the cops on him.

One way I learned to cope with the looming sense of some tragedy befalling my father was to immerse myself in other people's problems. My ministry at the church included working with adults with severe mental illness at the drop-in center housed in the church's basement. I instantly connected with this community because they were like family. I understood on a basic level why so many of them needed each other to be a family. Very few were on good speaking terms with members of their families of origin. Loving them was one way that I could love my father. The people in the drop-in group suffered from severe mental illness, but they navigated life fairly well by staying on their medications. Many of them lived in group homes and walked to the church or took the bus.

Ben had a 35 mm camera hanging from a thick strap around his neck and was always planning his next slide show. His favorite shots came from the IDS Tower, the city's tallest building. Liz was a tall, lanky lady whose face looked a lot like her pet parakeet. She sounded like her bird too—always screeching and flapping her arms around because something or other was missing or stolen. And then there was Frank, a rotund and soft-faced man who murmured through his smiling lips while holding hands with his girlfriend, who shared the same name as me.

Among the twelve or so regulars at the drop-in center, the slightest change in plans could cause great agitation and outrage. They found comfort, control, and normalcy in having a predictable schedule of activities each week. You should have seen them play bingo. The best part was when they'd eye the prizes lined up on the long tables as they first entered the bingo hall. Prior to every bingo game, our volunteers carefully laid out all of items donated by church members: XXXL-sized sweatshirts, clocks, flashlights, toiletries, and the like.

David not only attended the drop-in center, but came regularly to Sunday morning worship in the sanctuary. Every time I stood in the pulpit to preach, all I had to do was look down in the front pew, and there was David with a smile and an "Amen" for me. I will never forget the Sunday when my sermon about the rape of Dinah (in Genesis 34) opened the door for him to tell me about his own tragic childhood as a victim of incest. On Sunday mornings at church, in the midst of the lawyers and doctors in suits, David looked and smelled like a dumpster in a sports jacket, but it was a beautiful thing to see how he proudly claimed his identity as a child of God and took his seat at God's table.

Denying Communion

In the spring of 2002, I went to my brother Scott's graduation from UCLA with his Ph.D. in Biochemistry. I knew my dad still lived in L.A. and was planning to be at the graduation ceremony. I never knew what to expect with my father. I decided to see him in person, but only in public. I waited until I was in L.A. to call him, in case I changed my mind. By phone we arranged to meet up at the derelict gas station near my brother's apartment, and from there decided on lunch at the downtown diner next to the movie theater. Lunch and a movie sounded very normal. Even though my faith had helped me forgive him for hurting me, I was uncomfortable with the manifestations of his mental illness. For this visit I allowed a window of four hours, knowing that I could tolerate him in small doses, especially if half of it would be spent silently staring at a movie screen.

I was still anxious about facing him, because for most of my life he terrified me. His untreated bipolar disorder had intensified over the years and alienated him more and more from our family and society. Yet as an adult I felt more in control and empowered to call the shots, dictating the parameters of our contact. *This time, we will sit down at a common table together and break bread,* I told myself. *It doesn't have to be awful or scary, right?*

At the diner, he limped to the table. He seemed old and tired, dragging his right leg, and grabbing the edge of the table to prevent himself from falling. Twenty years before the bipolar disease disabled his mind, all the bones in his legs were shattered when a drunk driver ran him over as he walked home from work one late stormy night. It took him a year, nursed at home by his mother, to recover. And still he always had a limp. At six feet-plus, he was a giant compared to my petite five foot three. He seemed to fold himself in half as he squeezed into the red vinyl booth. His stomach barely fit behind the table. Looking at me, he smiled. *Who is this person,* I wondered. *He doesn't feel like my father, but more like the creepy guy down the street you barely know.* The table separating us helped me feel physically safe, and I kept an emotional distance from him too, wanting to protect myself.

Our food came to the table and we began eating our meal. Things seemed fairly normal until he blurted out, "I wanted to ask if you could do me a favor. Would you serve me communion?"

"What?" I asked, not quite sure what he was talking about.

"You are a minister now, aren't you? I haven't been to church in a long time and I would like communion," he said with a smile.

He cannot be serious. "You want me to give you communion right now in the diner?"

He was serious. He wanted me, his daughter, not his minister, to serve him communion at a diner, not in a church. *Why couldn't he go to church like normal people do when they want communion,* I thought to myself.

I made an excuse, anything to get me out of this one. "I don't think I can because I'll get in trouble," I said, in hopes that it would shut him up. He just laughed. It wasn't a complete lie. Technically the religious sacrament of communion is designed for worship within a community. The only time individuals took communion alone was because of a grave illness that kept them apart from the church. My father was sick, but not that sick.

Clearly he saw the world and me differently than I did. I wasn't just his daughter; I was now a minister, his minister. And in his mind it was perfectly normal to ask me to serve him communion at a diner. He asked me again to give him communion.

"Dad, let's go. It's time to get to the movies." I paid for our lunch and we slowly walked down the sun-splashed street to the movie theater. I bought two tickets for a matinee viewing of *The Perfect Storm*. Inside it was cool and dark. The seats were soft and I allowed my body to relax into the cushions. "I can do this. This is normal," I thought. I lost myself in the booming sound and flashing images, letting it carry me to a faraway place.

Dad showed up for the outdoor graduation ceremony at UCLA. He was dressed up in black pants and white dress shirt and tie, proud of his eldest son's accomplishments. Dad looked perfectly sane, and even happy. The crazy part is what came out of Dad's mouth during the reception after the graduation ceremony. Seated with my brother's in-laws (an interracial couple), he began to recount the history of the Ku Klux Klan and its impact on American politics. By now, my brother and I had both mastered the fine art of redirecting conversations, although not without some dismay and discomfort with the high level of inappropriateness Dad seemed to attain each time we met with him.

He Was There

In the early winter of 2004, while serving the church in Minneapolis, I met my husband Jonathan. After initially meeting online, our first face-to-face encounter was at an evening yoga class in St. Louis Park, followed by a sushi dinner. When we first started dating, I didn't tell him I was a minister right away. Instead I said something vague, like, "I help people in the community." In the past, prospective boyfriends had often assumed I must be celibate and not interested in sex or romantic attachment since I was in a religious profession. But Jonathan had no problem once he found out I was a minister, because he soon learned I was a sexual being as well.

My college experience of Christian community had profoundly shaped my understanding of sexuality as a young adult. As part of being born again, I was told that I needed to become a born-again virgin, vowing to refrain from sexual intimacy until marriage. One guy I dated during this time didn't believe in kissing until marriage. Another guy I dated believed that only kissing was appropriate until marriage. In this born-again dating culture, it was the guys who set the standard for what my sexual purity would look like. Yet, over time as I grew in my understanding of faith, I found this belief in sexual purity to be grounded in judgment and shame, not redemptive justice and love.

What really changed my belief was an experience of what I now understand to be sexual violence, regardless of the man's intention. As a poor college student without health insurance I went to the city's free clinic for my first pap smear. The exam room was a dirty and crowded supply closet with an exam table in the middle. The doctor walked in, and with no introduction or preliminaries about my health, jammed his cold, stiff fingers inside of me, and ignored my cry for him to stop. I left the clinic so emotionally distressed and heartbroken that my body could be touched so violently by a stranger. It didn't occur to me at the time to report the doctor's offenses to the authorities. The doctor made it seem like the pain was my fault and I felt powerless to stop him. The previous three years of college dating relationships had included closely guarding my body from any "inappropriate" touch. The lack of loving touch by people I trusted made this violation by a stranger hurt even more.

While studying in Glasgow, Scotland, for a semester my junior year in college I took the train to explore Rome for a week. While on a crowded city bus on my way to the Vatican a man standing behind me pressed up against me. At first I wasn't alarmed, as we were all touching strangers during a rush hour commute across town. But then his hand slipped in-between my thighs. I froze. I couldn't believe what was happening. Immobilized by fear I did not scream or even whimper. Within seconds I snapped out of it and jumped off the bus at the next stop, even though I had no idea where I was getting off. That night in my cramped hotel room I called a friend back in Texas, charging the call to a credit card (the bill was over $200) weeping over the feeling of helplessness and violation. What had happened to me and why? Did I somehow bring it upon myself? It felt like it was my fault, somehow. Yet now I know this reversal of blame is common among victims of sexual assault.

I worried that these experiences would later deny me intimate pleasure given by someone I loved. When I returned from studying abroad, I decided to take my body back: back from my born-again boyfriends and their stupid rules, back from the praise band chorus of True Love Waits, and back from someone else's idea of purity. My body needed me to love it all the way.

By the time I graduated from college, I was twenty pounds lighter, shaving my legs on a regular basis, and trusting my own instincts when it came to sexual intimacy. My relationship with my Father God, embracing my new life in Christ, liberated me to focus newfound energy on healing my entire self: body, mind, and spirit. By the time I became a minister, I embraced my body and my sexuality as a gift from God to be shared with the person I loved. After two years of dating in Minneapolis, Jonathan and I moved to Florida where I was called to be the pastor of a small congregation and he was hired by the local newspaper as a graphic artist. Soon after moving, Jonathan proposed to me on the Florida beach, following an afternoon of shopping and with ice cream still sticky on our fingers. We imagined ourselves exchanging vows on a cruise ship in the Caribbean; however, my mother talked us into a hometown wedding in Columbia, Missouri. She offered to help pick up the tab.

I had never dreamed of asking my crazy father to walk me down the aisle. But I panicked, trying to think of who would do the job in his place. He probably wasn't even going to attend, since nobody knew exactly where he was. So, I asked my oldest brother Scott to do the honors. Two days before my wedding, my father called from the local train station saying he needed a ride. How did that happen? I had sent a wedding invitation to his old address, but assumed he would never get the invite, let alone even come. The father of the bride was going to make it after all. *Should I ask him to walk me down the aisle?* I wondered for a moment. *No.* It wouldn't feel right to me. When my brother Scott found out Dad was coming to the wedding, he freaked out and told me he didn't want to walk me down the aisle if Dad was going to come. He said he was afraid of Dad and how Dad might react, making a big crazy scene because Scott was playing the part instead of Dad. We decided that all three of my brothers would walk me down the aisle because Scott said he would do it if the other brothers were with him. In a way, we were all protecting each other. These brothers were going to see that their little sister got married, with or without their father's blessing. Dad wasn't going to hurt us or stop our plans this time. Dad arrived on the train and Steve took Dad to buy new shoes and a suit for my wedding. Steve paid for Dad's hotel room and food. My brother made sure Dad got to the church on time.

All three of my brothers walked me down the aisle while my father sat in the back of the sanctuary by himself. After the ceremony he didn't come through the receiving line like the other guests. He was still sitting in his pew and remained there throughout all the after-wedding photography. We assembled for the traditional family photo: the new bride and groom, sister, brothers, and the mother of the bride, all trying to smile for the camera while just over the photographer's shoulder we could see my father sitting in the back pew by himself staring off into space. *Just say cheese and ignore him,* I thought. At the reception I went up to talk to him, but he covered his mouth while stretching his arm out toward me and said, "Don't get close. I don't want to get you sick. I'm so proud of you and I love you." That was it.

After the wedding, my father wanted to stay in Missouri and so he went to stay at his sister's house. That was short-lived. My aunt put him on the train with a one-way ticket just a few days after he arrived. Nobody in the family could stand to be around him for any length of time. Still, we could all tell by his shortness of breath that his physical health was rapidly declining, and we knew he would need care beyond what his roommate—if he had one these days—could offer. We couldn't abide the idea of him dying while living on the streets with no healthcare and no place to go. Soon after the wedding my brother Steve flew out to California and stayed for a week to arrange for our father to live in a nursing home. Our father acknowledged that he couldn't live in his truck forever, so he cooperated and moved into the nursing home. We found out later that my brother Steve paid for our father's care by taking a second mortgage out on his home.

Then He Was Gone

I spent the first weeks of the new year of 2007 as a newlywed on the other side of the planet from my groom. Having been invited to be part of a delegation of ministers to tour the Holy Land with all expenses paid, I could not refuse, even if the timing was bad. The political situation between the Palestinians and the Israelis was intense. Yet, my husband agreed that it was an opportunity not to be missed and that traveling with the delegation would be safe.

In Jerusalem our group visited the Western Wall, also known as the Wailing Wall. People throughout centuries have prayed, celebrated, and, yes, even wailed at this sacred site, the oldest known connection to the ancient Jewish temple. Pilgrims roll pieces of paper with their prayers written on them, and stick them into the cracks and crevices of the wall. I tore a corner of paper off of my itinerary. What was my one heartfelt prayer? I managed to scribble down the first words that came to me. Then, in humility and earnestness, I approached the wall (on the women's side) and tucked my prayer into one of the thousands of stone openings. My hole was at eye level and filled with miniature rolls of paper stacked one on top of another like pale bodies awaiting resurrection. My simple prayer was this: For my father to find peace.

Just months after my visit to the Holy Land, my father was dead. All I know was that he was hospitalized following a heart attack. None of us bothered with the inconvenience or expense of flying to the West Coast to visit him in the hospital or after he was discharged. The story goes that he was recovering quiet well and had been at a pizza party the night before his death. The following morning a nursing home staff person found him dead in his bed. They said that the night before his death, he was acting like his usual self, talking about getting his belongings back from the city impound and trying to recruit some helpers for the task. He ate pizza, had two cold beers and said goodnight. His friends at the nursing home said he was stubborn (their code word for crazy), but they liked him. They nicknamed him Santa Claus because of his big belly and white beard.

After my father's body was cremated we received a box with some of his papers, and his wallet with a twenty dollar bill in it. My brother Steve and sister Susan ordered pizza in memory of him. Among his papers was a First Communion certificate dated Easter Sunday 2006, from a church he attended in Long Beach. He finally got the holy sacrament that I denied him at the diner.

Learning of my father's death in the nursing home was strangely comforting. He did not die homeless. I was relieved that he died in a safe place. I was grateful that he was no longer suffering from his physical and mental diseases. Finally his broken mind and broken heart would be mended. These thoughts comforted me, but I still grieved—not just his death, but all the slow deaths along the way. He had missed out on us and we had missed out on him.

I told my congregation that my father died and that I needed to be away for a while to attend his funeral. They were surprised, saying "But he was so young." I received many sympathy cards from church members. The cards spoke of the pain of losing a beloved father, describing a father who was everything my father was not. The words made me feel worse, not better. They reminded me of all the father-daughter stuff that I had missed out on in my life. There should be a bereavement card that says, "Thank God that's over now."

But my congregation knew nothing about my father's mental illness, his deteriorating health, his ongoing affair with LaRouche, or his poverty and homelessness. I didn't feel it was search committee material, and over the two years that I had been with them it just never seemed appropriate for me to burden them with my personal family problems. It wasn't anything personal about this particular church; the people were caring and compassionate. I secretly feared that I'd lose my authority as a church leader if my congregation found out that my father, whose DNA is imprinted in my body and mind, had a severe mental illness. Maybe they would start checking my words and actions for indications that I was crazy too. I feared that if church members knew about my crazy in the blood, they would begin to treat me with what novelist Jeffrey Eugenides in *Middlesex* describes in the character of Father Mike as "a slight but unmistakable condescension, like a crazy person whose delusions had to be humored."[1]

I also didn't feel like I *could* tell the church the truth about the severe mental illness in my family. Christianity, with its starched white communion linens, didn't seem to want my blood stains on it. Jesus' blood was okay, but not the crazy blood that ran through my body. Ancient purity codes of the temple made menstruating women keep their distance and wash before re-entering society. Officially Jesus liberated the church from these restrictions placed on women and people with diseases, but in subtle and not-so-subtle ways, the church makes it known that nothing unclean should go near the altar. Women are still denied ministerial authority in many denominations, and people with diseases and disabilities find many churches to be unwelcoming, despite smiling greeters at the door. We mock Jesus when we reject people with mental illness because Jesus himself got crazy blood on his hands when he touched people with unclean spirits and exorcised demons from his followers.

My father's funeral was on a Sunday morning, at the little white country church where he grew up going to Sunday school in Clarksville, Missouri. The service began an hour before the regular worship service. We wanted to keep it simple for the Presbyterian minister, who we felt was doing us a favor. For the eulogy the preacher spoke appropriately about Don Quixote slaying windmills. My father's life didn't make sense and he was never understood. It must have been a lonely life. During the time for open sharing of stories and remembrances, none of the fifteen or so people there said a word. It was really awkward. As the "family minister" I had prepared something. I stood up and read a bad poem a friend gave me when, in desperation, I had called her asking for help. What was there to say? We are glad you are dead so you will stop driving us crazy and we can stop worrying?

My brother Steve dug out the Eagle Scout pin that my father had refused to accept—something about the Boy Scouts being part of a communist plot. At the graveside my brother ceremoniously placed the pin of honor into my father's cremains box to be buried with him forever. My father had no say in the matter.

Somewhere along the road, I think it was after my college graduation, my father had mailed me a gold Lady Liberty coin. At the time, I thought it was weird and tucked it away and forgot about it until he died. But now that he's gone, I realize that Lady Liberty is the only thing I have to remember him by and that what was once an embarrassing gift has now become a talisman. For his funeral I turned it into a pendant and bought a pure gold chain to hang it on.

I wore Lady Liberty as I said the words of interment at my father's graveside. My brothers and sister surrounded our father's open grave as I led the closing prayer, beginning with "Our Father, who art in heaven." As I said these words, they clung to my throat, huddling there like scared and abandoned little children.

chapter 3

Caring for My Brother—How Would Jesus Do It?

As a minister of God's word and sacrament, part of my job is to help people work through questions of theodicy— that is, "Where is God in the midst of suffering?" and, "Why do bad things happen to good people?" We all wonder this, and many of us ask the question readily when something bad happens. But what if the something bad is not an event—a car accident—but is instead something inextricable from our very being? "Why did God let me (or him, or her, or them) be born this way?" That's a harder one to ask because, in doing so, we seem to doubt God's appraisal of his own creation: "He saw that it was good." We hesitate to question God's goodness. Is God really good *all* the time, as the saying goes?

If we believe that God knits us together in our mother's womb, do we therefore believe that God knits crazy into our being? If God is in all places and is present at all times, is God also in mental illness? If we are made in God's image, then is God crazy too?

Or is mental illness one of those things Satan uses to undo us? When Jesus healed people who were mentally ill, he cast demons out of them. When Satan lured Jesus out to the edge of the cliff, he tried to make Jesus go crazy and jump. A case could be made that Satan, at the very least, has a knack for this kind of thing, regardless of whether he is actually at the root of it.

When I counsel people whose loved one has mental illness, I find that looking at it from a biochemical perspective helps. Brain chemistry influences our moods, emotions, and behavior. At its most basic, science has told us, mental illness is due to imbalances in brain chemistry. That is why drug treatment that alters brain chemistry is so often effective.

Yet this scientific approach does not let God off the hook.

Maybe, then, we could get some answers by a less direct route—say, storytelling. That was Jesus' teaching tool of choice. We've all got stories. You've heard part of mine. But there is more. In addition to being the daughter of a father with bipolar, I am also the sister of a brother with bipolar. My family's story of mental illness runs deep. To tell the story, to give my own testimony as the daughter and sister of crazy blood, is to slowly patch together pieces of my heart torn apart by pain and sadness of living with mental illness.

A Corruption of God's Law?

Some kids inherit natural good looks or a high IQ from their biological parents, and others get the crazy gene. Crazy in the blood runs thick in my family. The oldest boy, my brother Scott, seemed to get it the worst. The first-born son inherited, all right, just like in God's law, but instead of getting his father's blessing he got a curse.

As a young boy my brother Scott accepted Jesus as his Lord and Savior. He was a zealous child preacher, memorizing the Bible verses that promise salvation and blessing. He loved going to Sunday school and he reflected the love of Jesus back on the world like no other child or adult I knew. His white-blonde hair was like the light of Christ illuminating his face. But at some point the light began to fade and was replaced with something darker.

Over time my brother's experience of going to church changed. The change was due to more than just the intellectual doubts about God that adolescents go through as they develop critical thinking skills. Scott's experience of church, and Sundays after church most particularly, became tainted with violence.

Dad's physical and emotional abuse, formerly reserved for times when kids were acting out, crept into Sundays, and seemed to focus in on Scott, as if part of a bigger plan. I imagine that, for Scott, our father's hand came to represent the hand of an angry God, casting down punishment and fear.

Was Dad jealous that his oldest son had appeared to garner God's favor? Or had Satan possessed my father, causing him to take the holiest day of week, the Sabbath day, and make it a special occasion for child abuse? After church, our dad would force my brother, no longer a child, to pull down his pants and underwear, whipping him with a belt in front of us. All the footage from Dad's camcorder of my brothers playing basketball in our driveway after church, boys wearing Sunday best, cannot tape over the truth.

It didn't take long for Scott to put the two together: church and abuse. My brother's love for Jesus, like the flame of a candle, was swiftly blown out by our father's actions. Now as I look back, I wonder how this story would read if it really was Satan who caused my family's problems with crazy. What if the scientists have got it all wrong and crazy isn't passed on through the genes, but instead through the curse of Satan?

If it was Satan, then without the inner light of our Savior to guide him, my brother soon became consumed by other motivations. At school he was the model student, but at home he grew horns and a forked tail. Family games of Monopoly always ended with the board crashing down onto the family room floor and the miniature iron, shoe, dog, etc., flying everywhere, getting lost in the green shag carpet. My brother stomped around, cursing each of us, ensuring that no one but him ever won a game.

My father believed that his son's behavior was caused by a malformed spirituality. He would explain such outbursts as demonic possession, and eventually claimed that my brother was not only possessed by demons, but was himself a Satan worshiper. Dad blamed Scott for tearing apart our family. Scott quit attending church. He painted anarchy symbols on his bedroom walls, wore a spiked mohawk, and fiercely hated our father. I wondered whether Dad saw himself in Scott. Did he take any responsibility for the crazy in the blood that flowed in his offspring? Or was it easier to blame the devil?

During our first few months in Missouri after we left my father behind in California, my brother fell in love with a girl from school. He carved into the underbelly of his skateboard his beloved's name, along with a few other choice words: Kris is God. For my brother, this wasn't just some adolescent angst or poetic metaphor, as I first thought, but a profound truth that he discovered in her.

One day after school I made the mistake of answering the house phone and it was Kris. My brother wasn't home and I forgot to tell him she had called (this was the era before cell phones and text messaging). Later that night I was in my room trying on different outfits for the next day, trying to figure out which jeans made my butt look less fat. While looking in the mirror, all at once I heard a loud explosion and saw the mirror shake. My brother was at my door, kicking it with his steel-toed combat boot. "Why the f--- didn't you tell me she called?!!" The door was locked; he couldn't get in unless he kicked the door down. Safe for the moment at least, I fell to the floor crying.

I waited until I heard him stomping away, cursing me. Opening my bedroom door I saw at the bottom a big splintery hole just the size and shape of my brother's boot. My door. Broken apart. Like everything else. I found a piece of red cloth among my Girl Scout supplies. I got the scissors and cut from the cloth a larger-than-life heart. With wood glue from the garage I carefully arranged the red heart over the gaping hole in the door. *There. Now no one can tell how much it hurts. It is all covered up.* Covering up crazy and any signs of it became second nature for me, using whatever was handy.

We Thought He Would be Dead

Scott has made it to his fortieth birthday. By this time in his life, he thought he would be still married to his high school sweetheart. We thought he would be dead.

My brother experienced his first psychotic break and hospitalization during his senior year in high school. We guessed it was triggered by his girlfriend moving away to a university dorm across town. Scott did a series of bizarre things over a period of a couple of weeks, finally catching the attention of his school administrators the day he handed out large sums of his own hard-earned cash to other students on campus. Since Mom was teaching across town, Grandma picked Scott up from the principal's office that day, took him to her house and washed off the black paint he had smeared onto his own face before giving away all of his money.

It was the Monday before Christmas. I remember my brother in the kitchen screaming and crying. The police were there putting him in handcuffs. My mom was afraid he would kill himself. I don't know how she knew this, if he threatened or actually attempted it; but I do know that she did what she thought was best by calling the cops. And for decades afterward, Scott resented her for it.

Scott began the hard work of recovery and began to manage his bipolar through a combination of medication and psychotherapy. For a philosophy class senior project he posited the question, "If there was a happy pill that would make you happy forever, would you take it?" This question wasn't hypothetical for him, as it would be for most of the other students who had never spent the night in the hospital, let alone the psychiatric ward. No, for my brother, this was an issue of reversing the curse, the curse of crazy in the blood.

But in the absence of a happy pill, Scott had to struggle fiercely to face his demons. Along the way he married his beautiful and brilliant high school sweetheart Kris. He won full scholarships for his undergraduate and graduate education, earned his PhD in biochemistry from a top university, and got a college teaching position after his post-doctoral fellowship.

But by the end of Scott's time in graduate school, he suffered most days from major depression. Even though he and his wife lived just a short walk from one of the best surf spots on the West Coast, he couldn't get out of bed, let alone make the walk down the hill with his surfboard. That, he later told me, was his biggest regret: not surfing enough when he lived at the beach. Depression sucked any pleasure in life right out of him.

Scott's graduation was the highlight of his career. Once he got the teaching job, his medications were not working well and he couldn't really function. It was difficult for him to get to class in the mornings. He called in sick, and students complained that he was unfair in his grading, giving half the class a failing grade halfway through the semester. By the end of his first year he was fired. My brother tried suing the school for character defamation, but eventually that got dropped. Without a career he felt ashamed and lost, lacking any purpose or identity.

His marriage couldn't hold the weight of depression much longer. To confound things even more, Kris wanted a child, but she and Scott never agreed on the right time to start a family or whether it was even a good idea considering his health issues. He knew that there was crazy in his blood and he didn't want to risk passing the crazy on to another generation. Following the collapse of his career at the college, in 2005, Scott applied for federal disability benefits. When my mom and I first heard that Scott was considering applying to be on disability we thought it was a sign that he was giving up. In reality, we were in denial that Scott had a disability that was severe enough for him to qualify. We wanted to believe that if Scott only tried harder, he would be healthy again. Qualifying for disability, in our eyes, was like a death sentence, his life would be over. Yet for Scott, applying for disability was an act of courage. Scott told me later that the man who interviewed him to see if Scott would qualify said, "I commend you for being a strong person with an invisible disability. Everyone can see that I am disabled because I am in a wheelchair. But people can't see your disability." We were not as enlightened. The stigma of Scott's disability weighed heavily on us. We would now be the mother and the sister of someone who was mentally disabled. Now it was official. It seemed to be a turning point for all of us. My brother was legitimately crazy.

While Scott was visiting me in Florida one holiday, Kris called and told him she wanted a divorce. She had called me first to let me know what was coming, and to say that she didn't want Scott to be alone when she gave him the news. I told her that we were his family; we would take care of him. He stayed at my house for a few more days after that, but began obsessing more and more about killing himself. I hid our kitchen knives and scissors and removed all alcohol from the house. I let a few church members know what was going on, in case I had to respond to an emergency with my brother. And I asked them to pray for him.

Within the first month of Scott's separation, he went to the Mayo Clinic in southern Minnesota. Among the many things Mayo clinicians are known for is their expertise in treating organic brain disorders. That winter my mother drove an hour each way through the snow to have dinner with my brother and attend family sessions, which she reported were very stressful. During this time he got his medications straightened out, and learned that in order to accept the fact that his marriage was over, he would need to find a reason to live that did not include his ex-wife.

I remembered the rain that had come pouring down on Kris and Scott's wedding day and forced them to change the location from an outdoor setting at the river bluff winery to a stuffy indoor chapel at the women's college. They seemed so pleased with the Unitarian Universalist minister they hired because he promised them the ceremony would not have the word "God" in it. Over the years my brother and I have had ongoing conversations about the Bible and God. There was no reason to debate with him. I was neither intimidated nor offended by his unbelief, but rather enjoyed listening to his searching questions. He was fascinated at my choice to become an ordained minister. He was also proud of me and couldn't believe that I could preach every Sunday as if I really believed the stuff in the Bible.

Even though Scott claimed at that time to have no faith in a God, he was the most spiritual person I knew. For one thing,

Scott came the closest of all the five siblings to reconciling with our father. He sorted through all the emotional and physical abuse from childhood and eventually took pity on our father, reaching out to him, spending time with him. He tolerated our father's bipolar behaviors in a way that none of the rest of us could. I think it was because of the connection they shared. My brother saw how easily his own life could unravel and how he could become like Dad. By the end of our father's life, these two seemed to actually love one another.

In addition to that, no Christian I had ever talked with before questioned God, Jesus Christ, and the Holy Spirit with my brother's earnestness and sincerity. It wasn't until after he lost his job, his wife filed for divorce, and he moved to Florida to be closer to his siblings that he began attending a twelve step program on a daily basis, and found his Higher Power once again. He got his first Big Book at a meeting held at my church.

Through the support of the twelve step community, God emerged as a real presence in Scott's life, though he couldn't give a rational explanation for it. These days Scott testifies that his faith is shaped by his mental health. He explains it to me this way: when he is mentally stable he believes in God; when he is feeling manic he believes he is God; and when he is feeling depressed he believes there is no God. Daily attendance at twelve step meetings, in addition to keeping him away from alcohol, helps regulate his mind and spirit. The language of Higher Power was vague enough, hinting enough, hopeful enough, that it opened the door for him to be able to believe again. While churches were busy saving the world, AA kept busy saving the drunks.

More than once my brother has explained to me what it is like to live inside his brain. He has what is called suicidal ideation: several times a day he thinks about how to kill himself. He has fantasized, planned, and made arrangements for his own death since he was a kid. Some of his closest friends shared his obsession with death, including the best man at his wedding, who later committed suicide. During his marriage,

Scott overdosed a few times, combining deadly amounts of alcohol and pills. Thankfully, he had Kris to take him to the hospital. Scott has not directly credited God or his faith for keeping him alive, but he has noted that sobriety keeps him from following through on the suicidal thoughts. This is why I insist to my church that we will do whatever we can to open our doors to twelve step meetings. I believe that by so doing, we are realizing God's salvation, both in the sense of saving the lost and in the sense of providing salve, or healing, to people's lives. The spirituality of the twelve step program makes it the closest thing to church that many people experience. The last step of the program is a spiritual awakening.

Baby Jesus in Acute Care

In the summer of 2010, Scott moved to Florida to start over with the support of nearby family. Once while on our way to lunch, Scott pointed to a tall condominium on the river. He said, "As far as I can tell, that's the tallest building around here." When Scott said it, I knew immediately why that mattered so much to him. One of the symptoms of bipolar disorder is thoughts of suicide. He continually was on the lookout for buildings to jump off of and other ways to kill himself. Living with a bipolar brain disorder has brutally humbled him. It has cost him his career, marriage, house, physical health, friends, even his rescue dog Twinkie, who stayed with his ex in Missouri—and, according to mental health experts, he has the precise toxic mix for suicide: he's overweight, male, white, divorced, bipolar, and over forty.

He has tried to commit suicide many times, but the worst attempt, so far, happened three weeks before Christmas 2011.

Scott sat in his truck in the parking lot of Wal-Mart. On the seat next to him was a gun, plenty of bullets, and his will. That morning he had the will notarized and was leaving everything to our brother Steve. But then Scott realized how much dealing with the fallout from suicide would piss off Steve, so he called Steve first to apologize.

Scott had been drinking. Alcohol made the terror of taking his own life more tolerable. Yet even the alcohol could not keep him from worrying about how his death would affect his family.

So Steve, who lived nearby and is an emergency room doctor, talked with Scott on the phone until he was able to meet Scott at the Wal-Mart parking lot. Together they checked Scott into the emergency room.

I came to visit Scott the next day. No family visitors were allowed until later in the week, so I told the hospital staff that I was his pastor, not his sister. I carried my prayer book with me, to help me look more official. Pretending not to be siblings was hard. I could not hug him tightly when I saw him. Instead I shook his hand as the hospital staff looked on. I asked for some privacy to meet with him and they gave us a small office to sit in. I closed the door, leaving it open only a small crack, so that we could speak privately as brother and sister.

When we sat down, Scott smiled. I don't know what drugs he was on, or if he was still drunk or high. Or maybe he was sincerely happy to see me. He said he was embarrassed that he didn't go through with killing himself. He said he felt like a failure.

At one point during our conversation Scott toyed with the idea that suicide was a sin punishable with eternal damnation. But sitting in the psychiatric hospital, Scott said that God would understand the reasons he had for taking his own life. Inside I agreed with him. I don't claim to know what happens when we die. But I can't imagine a loving and compassionate God adding further punishment to a soul already tortured by mental illness. In my mind, God's forgiveness extends beyond this life. Whatever sins we may have committed, God is extravagantly generous in rescuing us from evil. I refuse to believe that people who commit suicide rot in hell for eternity. Instead of voicing those things, however, I told him how much God loves him. I wasn't ready to lose him at that moment.

From our conversations that night I felt strongly that my brother, if released from the hospital too soon, would immediately attempt to kill himself. The nearest safe place that accepted his insurance, a lockdown acute care treatment facility, was two hours away. We had him transferred there for a three-week stay. My mother and I went to see him the day after Christmas.

The acute care psychiatric ward was crowded and filled with stale air. A small TV blared in the common room. There was no sign or celebration of the Savior's birth here. If anything it was all that much worse because it was the day after Christmas. The staff looked bleary-eyed and half dead behind their computers. We went down the hallway and sat at a long table. Another family was there visiting a young man. The volume of their conversation quickly escalated to screaming, but there was nowhere else for us to go.

My mother tried to smile through the ugliness. She held my brother's hand. I don't remember what was said. It just seemed to be important that we were there.

Scott abhorred being there, like a prisoner on death row. He said his doctor was an arrogant, incompetent jerk. He wanted us to sign papers to release him under our care. My mother and I knew we couldn't do that. We still didn't trust that Scott would be safe outside of the hospital.

Thinking of that grim acute care ward at Christmas, I like to imagine Mom and me in the role of the magi coming to pay homage to the baby Jesus. We brought Scott our warm presence, our advocacy. He didn't want them, had no use for them. But like gold, frankincense, and myrrh, our gifts were for the person we knew him to be—a child of God, worthy of every one of God's promises, and nothing less. Scott was vulnerable and needed strength to escape his deadly impulses, just as the holy family fled to Egypt from murderous King Herod.

He called Steve and me several times a day, requesting we sign papers releasing him into our care. In the span of sixty minutes he left seven messages on my phone. If anything, we felt Scott might need to be in a care facility permanently. We wondered if he would be better off living in a group home for adults with disabilities. We were afraid that he was no longer capable of taking care of himself.

I missed work to attend the court hearing in which the judge officially ruled that my brother needed to be hospitalized against his will because he was at high risk for self injury. It was painful to sit there in the makeshift courtroom, a space in the wing of another mental hospital. My brother had requested that I give a testimony stating my belief that he in fact was of sound mind and not a danger to himself. It was hard, but I told Scott that I could not testify on his behalf, unless he wanted me to say that his family feels he was too high risk to be discharged from the hospital. I felt like a betraying sister, not a helpful one. I was sure that Scott would be angry and not want me to be there, but he seemed grateful to have me in the room with him at the hearing.

It was heartbreaking to hear the judge summarize my brother's case, defining him as mentally unstable to the point of losing his freedom. It confirmed our family's worst fears. Scott really was disabled. Scott was not going to be able to fulfill the dreams we imagined for him, like working in a top biochemistry lab discovering the cure to HIV/AIDS. His brilliant mind was slowly fading, and his personal life was falling apart. Where did he go? Where was he now? Had he changed so much now that he didn't exist anymore? Or was he still there, buried alive underneath the diagnosis and court ruling of insanity?

Dirtying Our Hands

Eventually Scott waited it out at the mental hospital and was released after finally getting permission from his doctor, who felt Scott had stabilized enough to be released under a family member's care with a plan in place for continued treatment. I agreed to be the one to look after him. In the meantime, I was trying to find another facility, a better one that would offer more help in his recovery. But he wasn't interested in any more treatment.

Once Scott was back at his apartment, I called him every day to check and see how he was doing. Was he going to twelve step meetings? Was he getting any sleep? Before his hospitalization, Scott co-facilitated Friday night twelve step meetings at the psychiatric ward, but since he was admitted as a patient himself, according to their guidelines, he had to wait six months before he could volunteer again.

Through Facebook and text messaging, I stayed in touch with his AA sponsor and roommates. They said Scott was drinking again. Then one night I called my brother and he sounded really drunk, talking in an exaggerated manner to disguise his slurred speech. He said he was in his truck, driving home.

I asked Steve to go check on him. When he did, he found Scott intoxicated, with more beer in the fridge, and with a bottle of empty pills. Steve had two choices: take Scott to the ER or call the police.

The police came and, after Steve showed them a photo on his cell phone of Scott's gun that he had bought to kill himself, they handcuffed Scott and took him back to the hospital. This time he stayed for a couple of days but was then released.

Today my brother seems to be at a "new normal," which is to say, he's alive but not thriving. The medications that he requires in order to stabilize his moods (and keep him from killing himself) have severe and devastating side effects. They make him crave food all the time, so he is fat. He is most often disheveled, with clothes that don't fit right and need to be washed. The meds also give him tremors, causing his teeth to chatter and his hands to shake. When we went to a Mexican restaurant for dinner one time, he kept spilling the salsa and queso dip on his clothes as he dipped his tortilla chips. He shuffles his feet when he walks, his muscles and motor skills impaired by the medications. He doesn't engage in witty conversations about politics or current events like he used to, his mind seemingly dulled now from disease.

At times Scott's meds have been so out of whack that he is like a zombie. Part of the problem is that Scott will experiment with different dosages of medication, creating his own cocktails of whatever medications he's collected over the years. And it doesn't help when he adds alcohol into the mix. Another problem is that his brain chemistry adapts to each drug so that over time the medication is less effective. More problematic still are the many side effects of his medications, including lethargy and dizziness. He cannot always control his behavior, like at my son's infant baptism when he decided to lie down on the cushioned pew. Other times he is like the Energizer Bunny on crack. Our mom recalls a time the first summer after Scott moved to Florida and he had a manic episode during a family vacation on a cruise ship. Scott had purchased a three-piece suit at one of the designer shops on board. Making large, spontaneous purchases is common during manic episodes. Then while at dinner Scott dumped thirteen chocolate mint candies into his entrée. They melted into his steaming pasta. It looked like diarrhea. Our seven-year-old niece leaned over and whispered into my mother's ear, "Sometimes it is embarrassing having an uncle like Scott."

When Scott went to Costa Rica to celebrate his fortieth birthday in August of 2012, we worried that he would not come back. He wanted to go alone. He once told me that the best way to kill himself would be to leave the country and just disappear. Our fears of him leaving the country were so great that had Steve confiscated his passport. But now that Scott had been sober for a couple of months, he had his passport back.

My mother and I were suspicious of Scott's birthday plans. I asked him more about them. Was there a local AA meeting he could go to? Was he taking all his medications with him? Was he planning on drinking while he was there? My mother was nervous about it too. She said her mother's intuition told her that it wasn't right. As it happened, my husband was able to go with Scott for the first part of the two-week trip. He kept Scott company and enjoyed some surfing as well, but then had to return a week before my brother was scheduled to come back.

Scott came back from Costa Rica alive, but attempted suicide again two months later. Just earlier that night he was at our sister Susan's new house, eating pizza with us around the swimming pool. But later he went out gambling and ended the night by swallowing a bunch of sleeping pills. He tried to smother himself with a drawstring bag, but panicked, took the bag off his head, and passed out. The next day his psychiatrist invoked the Baker Act, sending him to the local psychiatric ward for the third time in ten months. Getting "Baker Acted" means that a person is required to get an involuntary psychiatric exam, and this can be mandated by law enforcement, mental health professionals, or circuit courts.

Immediately following this episode, Scott admitted himself to a thirty-day inpatient treatment center that specializes in helping men with the dual diagnosis of bipolar disorder and addiction problems. I admired his courage and strength to ask for help even though we all knew he would rather die.

The Cross of Mental Illness

Loving a family member who struggles with mental illness is exhausting. One of the ways in which I have found support is through spiritual care from cherished friends and mentors. When I am afraid of impending catastrophe, I turn to them, give them an update, and ask for prayers. I pray to God for help. But more than help, I pray for peace, the peace that comes when I trust in God's goodness. The Serenity Prayer helps me to remember that there is so much I cannot control or change about the world, or about people.

Jesus seemed to be the exception to the rule. He changed people all the time. In one case, the diseased person simply reached out and touched the seam of Jesus' garment. Jesus said that people who want to follow him must take up their crosses. I used to think this was a curse, a sick punishment from God. But what if crosses just exist, like mental illness just exists? My brother did not make the cross of mental illness, but it is still his to bear. As his sister, it is mine to bear too. By bearing the cross of mental illness and carrying it, we can move it—not rid ourselves of it or deny it—to a place of transformation like Golgotha. On that hill the cross became something not to be despised but a thing to transform the world. The Christian witness of the cross of Jesus' death transforms this instrument of torture. Instead of only being the instrument that killed Jesus, the cross became a symbol of the power of God to overcome the sins of the world. In the resurrection, God shows us that what is broken by this world can be made whole again.

How can a cross of mental illness be transformed into a symbol of God's power to heal us? I believe that by telling our stories of mental illness, by giving our own testimonies for mental health, we carry our crosses to more healing places, even places of transformation.

When it comes to living with loved ones who are mentally ill, it is easy to waste energy worrying. We worry to cover up what we are really feeling: resentful, angry, afraid, anxious, hopeless.

One of the things I struggle with is learning to live with the limitations of not knowing what is going to happen and not being able to control my brother's behaviors. I have to let him live his life. What kind of life is it to be a grown man and have your motives constantly second guessed, to be what my brother calls "babysat" all the time? Sometimes all I can really do is pray.

The gift of prayer is that over time it can transform worry into something else. Spiritual transformation doesn't happen immediately, like creating light by striking a match. It is the day-by-day, hour-by-hour practice of lifting our worries up in prayer that brings about change. By taking our worries to God in prayer, we can free our minds. Prayer may not, in and of itself, cure disease, but it can be a balm, a comfort, and, most importantly, a way to survive.

Prayer changes my perspective. As C. S. Lewis once said, prayer doesn't change God, it changes us.[1] I heard Marjorie Suchocki, author of *In God's Presence,* speak at a church conference in Orlando where she said, "God works with the world as it is in order to bring it to where it can be. Prayer changes the way the world is, and therefore changes what the world can be. Prayer opens the world to its own transformation." She argues that prayer can even change God.

I can pray, but I realize that ultimately there is nothing I can do to stop my brother from killing himself. If he is determined to do so, then he will. I've learned that as Scott's sister, not his pastor, and certainly not his savior, I can make a commitment to carrying the cross of mental illness by doing these three things:

Love him (and tell him every chance I get);

Reach out to him;

Pray for him.

And, if I'm being really honest, sometimes I forget for a spell. A week or two goes by and I block all the crazy out of my mind. I try to forget all about the crazy in the blood by distancing myself from my family. I don't call or check in for awhile. I check out of the family madness and immerse myself in work, in nature, and in the things that bring me joy.

Yet, even then, a dull pain in my chest throbs, reminding me that in my heart pumps the same crazy blood...and I feel an aching part of me is missing. I pick up the phone and when I hear my brother's voice answer my call, my heart is warmed. Blessed are the crazy for we shall receive mercy.

chapter 4

Seeking the Holy Spirit on Death Row

"Ma'am, don't forget your Bible." These are the words the death row guard spoke to me immediately following my cousin Paul's execution. He said them as easily as if he were speaking to an elderly woman sitting in the pew next to him at church. On the makeshift raised platform, my Bible lay next to the bolted-down legs of my white plastic lawn chair.

Sitting here with my sister Susan and brother Steve, we had front-row seats to the big show. Once they opened the mini-blinds, we could see straight through the window into the execution chamber. Where was the popcorn? Everything was prepared, staged, timed, and programmed to the finest detail, like a sacred ritual—something of such great importance and done so frequently, yet whose meaning was not diminished by the repetition, but rather strangely strengthened in power each time. Like the sacrament of Holy Communion for Christians, the ritualized and communal experience of reenacting Jesus' body broken for the forgiveness of sins, execution was promised to be the greatest hope the victims had for...everyone wanted to believe that killing my cousin would make things right, somehow better than they were now.

If God exists, then where is God to be found during an execution? With the grief-stricken family members of the long-ago deceased? With the death row staff, the hard-working nurses and guards, who carry out the state's commandment to kill? With the one being executed? Or with the family of the one about to die?

After witnessing my cousin's execution that day, I had the answer to my primary question of God's whereabouts: for me at the moment of execution God was nowhere to be found. I felt a terrifying sense that I just witnessed the death of God.

Strength from Silence

I first learned of my cousin's execution date during my last semester of training for the ministry in seminary. My best friend from college Naomi (considerably less Jesus freakish by now) and I had just completed a silent meditation retreat hosted by the brothers of the Holy Cross Monastery on the Hudson River in upstate New York. Brother Bede led the retreat using the technique of mindful meditation. The idea is to sit, walk, eat, and breathe with intention and purpose. To do these simple bodily functions in silence heightens our awareness of the present moment. With awareness we can focus on God, in solitude, in the perfect moment of quiet peacefulness, away from the demands of the noisy world. I loved the easy way in which Brother Bede, a boyish seventy-something, taught us the spiritual practice of meditation. He's the author of the widely known booklet, "Using the Jesus Prayer." Perhaps living the monastic life since the age of twenty-five allowed him time to perfect the art of stillness, prayer, and opening the spirit to all that is holy.

A week of silence for me meant no cell phones, no e-mail, nothing from the outside world. I was beginning to understand that for me to be grounded, to have anything resembling an authentic spiritual life, I needed extended time, twenty-four hours at least, in silence. Once the retreat ended I reluctantly packed up my things and got ready for the long drive back to seminary. It was hard to break out of the cocoon of silence I had built around myself. Instead of craving human communication, I longed for more time with the silent divine. Sitting in my car parked in the monastery gravel lot, I checked messages, hypersensitive to the annoying sounds that came out of my cell phone. There was a message from my sister. She only calls with bad news. Little did I know that the week spent in silent retreat was preparing me for something I couldn't have imagined in my worst nightmare.

My sister said the local radio station had announced, like a sports event, the upcoming execution date for our cousin Paul. Sentenced to death ten years ago at the age of twenty, he was now slated to be executed by Easter Sunday. Paul was thirty years old, and the thirty-day eviction notice had been served.

A Killer, Born or Made

From the pieces my siblings can put together, it appears that Paul spent his first three years of life subjected to physical and sexual abuse severe enough for the state to remove him from his birth family, no relation to our family. It's ironic that the state, early on, played such a significant role in trying to save his life, only to end it a few decades later.

Paul, his twin brother Peter, and their younger sister Lizzy all ended up in foster care. The kids were a mess. That's how Aunt Carol, my dad's sister, found out about them. She was a social worker and knew these three kids had experienced hell on earth. So she adopted them.

Aunt Carol lived on the family farm in the rolling hills of the Missouri River valley, where she, my dad, and our uncle were all born and raised. Her house stood on a hilltop with a dilapidated red barn next door. The farmhouse was in such disrepair that Aunt Carol and Uncle Phil lived in a trailer on the property. They raised pigs, chickens, and cows. Our grandmother lived down the hill on a patch of farmland, and in-between them stood a weathered little white Presbyterian church.

We visited for a week every summer. We were city kids from Los Angeles running around with our farm cousins. We sometimes stayed at our grandmother's house, sleeping on couches or on the floor. Other summers we stayed in Aunt Carol's farmhouse. We thought it was part of the novelty of farm life that the house had no electricity or running water. The rooms we slept in were up the creaky staircase on the second floor, and the bedroom walls were covered in hundreds of daddy long leg spiders.

Down the hill at Grandma's, I loved peeking around the barn for kittens and wild strawberries. It was thrilling to tinker with the manual hand pump, and seemed to me a miracle to drink ice-cold water from the well. I can still see, smell, and taste the spread of food that covered the long table in the kitchen: homemade rolls, chicken noodle soup, and pink lemonade.

The beauty of the land and the wholesome work of taking care of it may have helped my adopted cousins make a new life for themselves. Yet, Paul never recovered from his early childhood trauma. Aunt Carol home schooled the kids on the farm, presumably because Paul and his siblings had learning disabilities and low intelligence. Yet she disciplined them severely. Her response to Paul's hyperactive behavior was to routinely withhold food and baths from him.

By the time Paul hit puberty he started to display an unhealthy obsession with sex and show early signs of sex addiction. It's possible that the childhood abuse Paul experienced triggered his deviant behavior. First it was pornography that he would proudly show to my brothers. He had it hidden out in the barn. When Aunt Carol learned about the porn, she had all the kids stand naked and spit on their genitals. It was only a matter of time before Paul was caught molesting his sister. Aunt Carol instructed him to have sex with cows instead.

Disgusted with Paul's deviant behavior, my aunt found what she saw as a solution. She locked him with a heavy dog chain to his bed at night. And when she didn't see positive results from that, she locked him in a wooden box (imagine a steamer trunk) with a padlock. So he would know just how dirty his little fingers were for molesting his sister, she pinched them with metal pliers. She smacked him with fly swatters and planks of wood. Paul wet the bed and she punished him by making him drink his own urine. None of these activities—Paul's misbehavior, Aunt

Carol's attempts at discipline—were reported to the authorities, but kept as family secrets.

Realizing that he was out of control, Aunt Carol sent Paul to a local boys home. There, the state classified Paul at the age of 14 as an abused and neglected child. But things were no better for him there. He acted out abusively to the other boys, and during one of his attempts at running away, he stole a tractor from the farmer who owned the adjacent property.

Later, when we moved to Missouri, we didn't visit my dad's sister Carol or my adopted cousins anymore, and I knew to stay away from Paul. He was kind of creepy. He had long stringy blonde hair, light blue eyes, and this crooked grin. When I was in high school, Paul was arrested and found guilty of indecent exposure. After he got out of prison, my mom and I came home one afternoon to find Paul parked outside our house in his old white sedan waiting for us. He said he needed some gas money to get back to the farm. My mom gave him a twenty and he was gone.

Two days later we heard on the news that a 36-year-old woman named Barbara, a wife and mother of three who lived less than a quarter of a mile from my grandmother's farmhouse, had been brutally raped and murdered. Paul was the suspect. They found bloody clothes in the trunk of his car, along with the baseball bat he used to beat her and the belt that he used to strangle her to death. According to public records, the officers who arrested Paul that night found him in possession of the victim's wallet, as well as a pair of bloody gloves, a roll of duct tape and a BB gun. The boot prints on the outside of the victim's bedroom door matched Paul's combat boots. He never denied the allegations and DNA analysis of the semen on Barbara's body had him nailed.

Was Paul a natural born killer? Perhaps. But I can't help but wonder how any killer instincts he may have been born with were encouraged with each pinch of the pliers, each click of the padlock, each pang of hunger, and each smack of the wooden plank. Court documents from his trial summarize Paul's fate this way: "The hopelessness of his childhood would predict the course of his life, as brief as it has been so far."

The state tried to rescue Paul from his abusive home and mentally ill parents. But in his adopted home his caregivers continued to abuse and neglect Paul, his twin, and his younger sister. My family had witnessed the abuse but did nothing to try to change it. It seemed to be a strange part of country life. It was also familiar to us—even, in a sense, normal—because of our own sick and abusive father.

The Messy Logic of the Law

At the murder trial, Paul was represented by a state-appointed attorney, but the case was a done deal. At the age of 20, when other young adults are in college and looking forward to receiving diplomas, Paul received a death sentence. According to court records, at trial he relied on a defense of "diminished capacity," claiming that he suffered from a mental disease." Paul's defense testified that the murder was not premeditated, but an impulsive response to a deep reservoir of anger linked to his mental illness.

To those ordinary citizens who heard Paul's testimony, it wasn't enough that he was the victim of abuse since birth. It didn't matter to them that a psychologist testified that he suffered from post-traumatic stress disorder, depression, sexual identity disorder, identity disorder of childhood, borderline personality disorder, and a schizoid personality that resulted from past physical and emotional abuse. It didn't matter that he was experiencing a psychotic episode at the time he committed the crime.

It didn't matter that the night of the murder, before Paul was arrested, he helped a young woman who was stranded with a flat tire. What mattered to the jury was that Barbara was dead. Not only had Paul raped and murdered her, but he had also taken her wallet, which contained twenty dollars. The jury found Paul guilty, knowing the judge would sentence him to death and not to life in prison, because he committed murder while engaged in burglary, a felony. Twenty dollars literally cost Paul his life.

There was no doubt that Paul was a killer. In the eyes of the law, it didn't matter if Paul was born that way or raised that way. And so, according to the laws of the state of Missouri, he should be killed: an eye for an eye.

To my adolescent mind this logic made good sense. It was obvious there was something seriously wrong with Paul. His criminal record included burglary and robbery, yet who was to say he wouldn't kill again and become a serial killer? Execution ensured that he would never hurt anybody ever again. It also ensured that no one could ever hurt Paul again—no more broken bones, no more abuse, no more physical, mental or emotional torture, except, depending on your take on God, in hell. Perhaps executing Paul would be the best thing for everyone. And so I made up my mind. Paul was getting what he deserved. I soon forgot about him.

It wasn't until my junior year in college that I even remembered I had a cousin on death row. I had erased him from my life. It was easy and painless to do. But then I heard Sister Helen Prejean speak at my college about her work to abolish the death penalty. Her riveting written account, which was made into the major motion picture *Dead Man Walking,* had gotten a lot of people talking again about capital punishment. Her story inspired me to look at my own story. My life's story included death row too. I was ready to face it.

The Spirit in Lockdown

I began writing letters to Paul on death row. I wanted him to know that I had not forgotten him after all. I shared with him about how during college my faith became central to my life.

He wrote back sharing that he was so thankful to hear from me. He wanted to know how everyone in my family was doing. He also shared his faith with me, saying that he got saved too. During his time on death row he gave his life to

Christ, asking Jesus into his heart. Now Paul zealously studied scriptures, wrote religious poetry, and drew pencil sketches of his spiritual visions.

Paul shared his personal testimony with me through his letters from death row. His letters spoke about the amazing grace he found in Jesus and how this brought him great peace of mind. He said it was no picnic to be on death row and that he often preferred solitary confinement, making special requests to remain isolated.

Hearing about Paul's transformation made me reconsider my view on capital punishment. So dramatic was Paul's change of heart that I began to question whether the person the state would eventually execute was the same person who committed the murder. Did this new, born-again Christian still deserve to die? Did God save Paul, giving him another chance in life, even if the state would not?

Other members of my family also began reaching out to Paul, including my brother Steve and sister Susan, who wrote him letters and visited him. My other two brothers simply wished to have nothing to do with Paul. The whole thing was too messed up for them to wrap their minds around. My father, meanwhile, was convinced of Paul's innocence. My father believed that Paul was framed by the government as part of the communist plot to overthrow his family. I still thought Paul was guilty, but I wanted to honor him as part of my family.

Believing in Paul's sincere relationship with Jesus Christ, I said yes when he asked me to be his spiritual director. His execution was scheduled during the week leading up to final exams. I spoke to my seminary professors, asking permission to miss class in order to go to death row. Victor, a seminary administrator, said, "Sarah, you must go, and there you will find holy ground."

My boyfriend at the time organized a candlelight vigil on the steps of the seminary's Miller Chapel to take place during Paul's execution. Knowing that my friends and people I didn't even know were praying and lifting up a light in the darkness was the only thing that gave me spiritual comfort during the execution. Afterward, when I returned to campus, I offered to give my testimony of what it was like to witness my cousin's execution. I expected only a handful of listeners but instead found the lecture room filled with students and professors. Among the audience were many international students who were incredulous that America, a beacon of freedom and liberty in the world, would execute its own citizens. One said to me in a quiet voice, "I can't believe this happens here in America."

On the day of Paul's execution I went to the prison. In order to see him, I passed by armed men standing watch outside the electric fence, in the parking lot, and on the prison roof. Inside I went through a full body scan that required me to remove layers of clothing. I felt like I was entering a dungeon, a true pit of despair where there was no air to breathe, even though the walls were bleached white and floors sparkling clean. The district coordinator of the prison chaplaincy program greeted me after the security check. He was surprised and happy to learn I was a Princeton Seminary student and he encouraged me to consider going into prison ministry. Annoyed, I swept past him. My cousin was about to be executed! If I ever felt called to prison ministry I was deaf to it at that moment.

When it was time to see Paul, I followed an armed guard through several more layers of security, going down long hallways, elevators and through thick bulletproof doors. Each level of security that I passed through felt more and more removed from the light of the world. Paul waited the last 36 hours before lethal injection in an 8 x 10 foot holding cell. He wore thin, white cotton pants with an elastic band, a white cotton T-shirt, and white canvas shoes with rubber soles. His blond hair was now short and his black framed glasses pressed into the crown of his nose.

Terrified, I sat down across from his cell. His cage. I was instructed not to cross the red line taped onto the floor. No handshake, no hug, no touch was allowed. Forbidding human contact with a loved one in the hours before execution seemed an unnecessary tragedy to pile on top of the ultimate punishment.

Paul was allowed to make phone calls, and he could request movies to watch and favorite foods to eat. For his last meal he requested a grilled ham and cheese sandwich, onion rings, and milk. He requested chocolate cake for his last dessert, but was given cheesecake instead. The meal sat untouched. The nurses were starting to worry about him because he wasn't eating. They offered him higher dosages of anti-anxiety and antidepressant medications. The prison staff was still charged with providing care to Paul even as they prepared the injections that would soon kill him.

The time for family visiting hours ended at lunchtime on the day of the execution. But as Paul's spiritual advisor, I was granted the privilege of extra time to be with him during the last hours of his life.

One of Paul's final requests was to be reunited with his biological mother and father. He wanted to face them both and ask them why they treated him and his siblings so badly. Paul wanted them to take some responsibility for causing so much pain and trauma in his early life. By some miracle, they were tracked down and contacted. They agreed to come visit Paul on death row. I came the day after their visit. When I asked Paul how the visit went, he said he was glad they came, but that it didn't change the way he felt about them. They were still doing drugs, still irresponsible. They had ruined his life forever. And there wasn't anything that could be done about it now. Instead of being angry, Paul seemed sad and disappointed.

Sitting across from Paul's death row holding cell I asked him how he was feeling. He admitted to feeling nervous. He believed that his execution would be cancelled. He hoped that his state-appointed lawyers would be able to intervene on his behalf. Yet when it became clear as the minutes ticked away that his life was about to end, Paul withdrew into himself. He refused to give any last words to be read upon his execution.

In the final moments, he was no longer interested in talking to me about his visions of heaven (riding a Harley Davidson over the hills, or riding horses with our grandpa—public record stated that the reason Paul visited his victim's home the day of the murder was to look at a horse they listed for sale). Instead, I watched as he curled up in a little ball, in a fetal position, seeking comfort he never knew in this life. His bed was a thin wood box, not unlike the box from the days of his childhood torture. By the end of my visit with him, he no longer wanted to talk. For a good while we shared the holding cell space in silence, me praying with each trembling breath.

The nurse said it was time for me to go. So before I left I said the Lord's Prayer and read to him his favorite poem, "Footprints." My last words to him were, "Know that I love you and God loves you too."

From here the guard took me to another waiting area where I joined my brother Steve and sister Susan, who came at Paul's request. Paul asked his twin brother Peter and his younger sister Lizzy to come witness the execution, but they decided to wait outside in the parking lot. They just couldn't bring themselves to watch.

Paul's adopted mother, my Aunt Carol, was in the waiting room along with her oldest son. We waited for what seemed hours, though I'm sure it was no more than 30 minutes. My aunt asked me to say a prayer for the family while we waited. I wanted to leave. I didn't feel like praying. But I muttered a quick one anyway.

Justice That Does Not Restore

When it was time for the execution, the guards walked us to the viewing platform. The family of the victim was also waiting to watch Paul's execution, but they waited in a different room. Their viewing platform was on the other side of the execution chamber. Everything is designed so that the two families never have contact with one another. They use different entrances into the building. The prison complex is in a rural area, four hours' drive from the nearest city, so families often choose to spend the night before the execution in a hotel. The prison staff even ensures that the two sides stay in separate hotels.

Sitting in the second row, I put the Bible on the floor next to the chair and folded my hands in my lap. In front of me was a small window covered with closed white mini-blinds. Then on a loudspeaker a man's deep voice announced the execution would begin in five, four, three, two, one. Suddenly, the mini-blinds flipped open. Inside I saw Paul lying on a hospital gurney. In a split second, Paul turned his head to look at us through his thick glasses and then his pale blue eyes shut.

As the lethal chemicals moved through the IV, the muscles in Paul's arms twitched. His face began to turn pale and his bare chest stopped moving up and down. Never before had I witnessed a perfectly healthy young man's body suddenly stop working. It was 1:01 a.m.

It felt like I had just witnessed a murder. Many states switched to lethal injection, in part because it was deemed more humane, less brutal, and less painful than the electric chair or a firing squad. Yet for me, it felt as if blood had splattered everywhere. This was a crime scene.

Call the police! I wanted to shout through the tears streaming down my face.

Instead, the mini-blinds were swiftly closed. The show was over.

We were ordered to leave immediately. Before the execution I had been told that, as his family, we would have time to sit with his body. They lied.

Instructions were given that we would be escorted out of the building, into a van, and taken to our cars in the parking lot. I got up to go feeling betrayed, confused, and nauseated. The guard reminded me not to forget my Bible. I snapped back, "Don't forget Paul."

We spilled out of the van next to our cars. There Paul's twin Peter and sister Lizzy stood waiting in the dark. Near them were two nuns holding candles and a sign that read, "An eye for an eye makes us all blind." Peter came running up to me, grabbed me, and began sobbing on my shoulder. I held his shaking body. His twin brother had just been executed. They say that twins have a bond stronger than any other. What of the horror could he feel? Peter went missing after that and to this day we do not know where he is.

The drive home was silent. So was God.

Paul's wasn't the only death that night.

Sure, I was able to grab my Bible from off the floor and bring it home with me. But my faith in God stayed behind, this time not because I'd chosen to drown it, but because it got caught in the cement corridors of death row, trapped in the plastic tubing that carried a toxic mix of chemicals into my cousin's body, and stuck to the yellow teeth of the prison chaplain who smiled at me.

There was nothing I could have done to help Paul. I was powerless to save his life. It turns out that God couldn't really save his life, either. The great machine of the criminal justice system did what we created it to do, but this did not, I believe, serve the purpose of God's law. God's law restores. God's justice gives life. The family of Paul's murder victim was interviewed about the execution on the evening news. Barbara's husband said, "It didn't bring back my wife. I am still going to go home tonight and she is not going to be there."

Barbara's family was let down by the state and the promised redemption that was to come from the execution of the killer. Paul's death did not restore life to anyone—not Barbara, not her three children, and not her husband. The only successful outcome of the retributive justice model of capital punishment is just that...punishment. In the aftermath of a crime most people think of justice as punishment. Restorative justice is an alternative model becoming more popular throughout the U.S.A. It strives to address the necessity of healing for not only the victims, but the criminal as well. Restorative justice is a global movement intended to balance the needs of both victims and offenders by reconciling relationships. My first experience with restorative justice was as the Minister for Outreach working with a neighborhood association in Minneapolis to address neighborhood crimes. It is an inclusive model of justice that views both the innocent and the guilty as candidates for redemption. This model closely follows Jesus' teachings to love our enemies and travel the long, difficult, but humanizing and liberating road to reconciliation. Restorative justice is the best hope for a society that is committed to ending the cycle of violence.

The introduction to Paul's petition for clemency quoted a statement made in 2000 by the U.S. Conference of Catholic Bishops. It read:

> Capital punishment...fails to live up to our deep conviction that all human life is sacred. The antidote to violence is love, not more violence... We are asking whether we can teach that killing is wrong by killing those who have been convicted of killing others... We cannot overcome crime by simply executing criminals, nor can we restore the lives of the innocent by ending the lives of those convicted of their murders. The death penalty offers the tragic illusion that we can defend life by taking life.

Truth-Telling in Tongues

Having a family member on death row made it easier for me to understand how people end up in prison. A good attorney could have gotten my cousin a life sentence instead of death. But Paul fit into society's category of "throw away"—he was a young, poor, mentally ill, uneducated man with a criminal record reaching back to early adolescence. More often than not the final verdict depends on how much money you have to fight in the courts.

After the execution, I began to feel more and more unsettled by what had happened to Paul. So much so that even though I was training for the ministry, I began to apply to law schools. I thought that I could work within the criminal justice system to change the laws. I studied for and took the LSAT. I spent hundreds of dollars on a dozen or so law school applications.

Looking back, this was good therapy for me. My law school application included an essay testimony about my cousin's execution. My testimony and LSAT scores didn't get me into any law schools (I was wait listed at one), but it did give me something to do with my confusion and pain.

In 2004, two years after Paul's execution in Missouri, I had a chance to give my testimony at a Minnesota Senate hearing when they were considering reinstituting the death penalty. I wore my clergy collar and told the story I have told you here. "How can our authorities, in the name of justice, carry out such calculated terror?" I asked those present at the hearing. "Why do we kill our own citizens to show that killing people is wrong? Isn't this just another form of revenge, and did we not create a justice system to free us from destructive cycles of revenge among clans and tribes?" By the end of my testimony I was physically shaking. Giving my testimony was a powerful way for me to redeem the traumatic experience of witnessing my cousin's death. I had done it during seminary for the scholars and pastoral leaders; I had done it for myself in writing law school admissions essays; and now I wanted the people in power to know that murderers have families too. The effort to reinstate the death penalty in Minnesota failed by a vote of eight to two.

As I gave voice to my own experience for a third time, I found God's Spirit coming back to me. Over time I came to believe that God was there on death row all along. As Paul's spiritual advisor, God was with me, working through me, yes. But God was also in Paul, a redeemed sinner.

God did not abandon me and God did not abandon Paul. But another question remains: if God was with Paul and in Paul, then what happened to the God-part of Paul when he was executed? Did part of God get executed too?[1]

This is what makes the most sense to me now: part of me and part of God died the night of Paul's execution. And I wonder if each execution has a cumulative negative effect on the prison staff who work intimately with the death row inmates. The prison nurses had a dual role to both care for Paul in his years on death row—to treat any illness, such as sinus infection, migraine headache, even clinical depression—and to prepare him for his death. In these cases, what happens to the Hippocratic Oath that medical professionals make, promising they will do no harm?

Paul's execution was one of the last in Missouri to take place at the same facility as death row. They now send the inmates to a separate facility for the actual execution. That way the nurses and staff involved with the execution have no personal relationship that has developed over a long period of time with the person being executed. There is no human connection. It is easier to kill that way.

About a year and a half after Paul's execution, while I was serving the church in Minneapolis, I began having flashbacks and nightmares about the execution. During a session with my spiritual director I said that the execution was a traumatically transformative experience in my life, but beyond that I could not articulate how it had changed me. My symptoms were the same as the post-traumatic stress disorder common among people in combat zones.

To sort through these thoughts and feelings, I began working as a chaplain in a local women's prison. I'd done what I could about the death penalty for the time being by testifying, writing, and preaching about it. Slowly my heart and mind were healing. Now I could struggle with the tension between prison as a place of punishment and as a place of healing. The women had very limited personal freedom, yet they were offered balanced meals, twelve step meetings, Bible studies, doctor visits, and continuing education.

What was the role of faith in helping the prisoners to heal and overcome the obstacles to their independence? As their chaplain, I felt like the most I could do for them was to listen to their stories and hear their own testimonies of faith. The women confided that at night when all the lights went out, they spoke to each other through the openings in the outlets in the walls of their adjoining cells. Talking to each other—sharing their feelings, giving their testimonies, and expressing the fears that kept them awake at night—all this was essential to keeping them from going crazy.

One of the inmates always insisted on praying for me. Allowing her to do this took me to a disorienting place, as though hearing the ravings in that Pentecost gathering when the Holy Spirit broke into the room with rushing wind, tongues of fire, and a babble of languages. In that odd place I found the courage to once again ask the question: Where is God in the prison? The inmates taught me to see that God is in the guilty ones, the sinners, the outcasts, and the ones that society rejects and throws away.

As a Christian I want so badly to believe that God has the power to save us. But what life has taught me is that God cannot save us from situations where we choose to give fear and hatred power, and, in so doing, choose other gods. When we choose the God of love, whose very nature is to reconcile all things, then we have a real shot at saving the world through Christ. Salvation means wholeness and it comes through relationships, not through individual piety. While shopping for groceries during Holy Week, I returned to my car and found a "ticket to heaven" tucked under my windshield wiper. It was a piece of white paper with instruction for what to believe in order to get to heaven. The problem with this logic is that it lets us off the hook because it doesn't require enough of us. God asks us to do more than simply believe. God asks us to follow the way of reconciliation, justice, and love. Too many Christians claim to be saved, yet in their support of capital punishment, they follow the way of vengeance, denying the God of love.

It is time for Christians to acknowledge that every time we execute a human being created in the image of God, we crucify God. Paul was a child of God, a person in pain, suffering from mental illness, desperately longing for wholeness and salvation. In response to his cries for help and psychological distress, we executed him. In response to Paul's violent acts, we acted violently to end his life. Violence, in whatever form it takes, carried out by individuals or society, cuts deeply into the human heart and the blood that is spilled seeps into the depths of the Earth's soil, becoming part of everything; the cycle of violence is never ending.

As a Christian minister who celebrates the sacrament of communion, and in light of my life experiences with victims of violence, it's become more difficult to swallow "the blood of Christ shed for me." Instead, I receive and offer to others "Christ's cup of love" as an affirmation of God's desire for all of creation to be made whole in love. I refuse to continue the tradition of the church that supports the use of violence as a means of redemption.[2] At first Jesus' death terrified his followers and signaled defeat of their kingdom building mission. It took several days before the disciples realized that nothing could separate them from the love of God in Christ Jesus, not even death on a cross.

If we are saved, it is only through God's resurrection grace and willingness to renew and restore creation. The resurrection is radically inclusive, offering new life to all, not just to some. We don't get to choose who gets to be saved.

After Jesus was executed by the authorities, his body was taken to a nearby garden tomb, anointed with oil and wrapped in linen cloths. When the poor are executed on death row, their bodies are destroyed, disposed of, and discarded by the state. In our case, there was a question about who could afford to claim and pay for Paul's remains. As with his birth and as with his death, Paul's body remained unwanted and abused by the world.

Lord, forgive us, for we do not know what we do. Blessed are the executed, for they will see God.

chapter 5

Feeling Pain in God's Presence

J esus, who carries the suffering of the world in his heart, is lifted up and surrounded by the white light of God. This vision flooded my mind one Texas autumn afternoon while I was walking to the campus cafeteria from my freshman dorm room. It was soon after giving my life to Christ that it came, knocking me to the sidewalk. And I wept at this vision of Jesus, the revelation of a God who embraced the world's pain and wrapped it in healing light.

I have come to believe that life's most difficult moments, when we feel as if God is very far away, are the times ripest for spiritual growth. Not because God is a sadistic puppeteer who is entertained by our suffering and takes pleasure in our pain. More like, in the words of Jewish and Buddhist mystic Leonard Cohen, "There is a crack in everything; that's how the light gets in."[1] In the midst of our pain we become aware of our frailty and vulnerability, our mortality, and our finitude, and in this state of weakness and helplessness we discover our empowerment to make a choice. We can choose God, above and beyond everything else. Spirituality is making the conscious choice to seek God's presence at all times. When pain breaks open our hearts, there is a new opening for God's light to enter in.

God's light is a welcome thing in our world of shadows. Psalm 23 describes God's presence with us even as we "walk through the valley of the shadow of death." The psalm says, "I will fear no evil, for you are with me." Just because we cannot feel God's presence does not mean that God is not with us. This is the hardest part.

In my ministry, people often speak to me of their struggle with believing in a truly loving God because, if such a God existed, then why, they wonder, is there so much suffering? In the face of a terminal diagnosis or the sudden death of a child, the pain can be so intense that it blocks all other feelings. Times of extreme suffering can be accompanied by an emotional numbness or feelings of fatigue. So what happens when we cannot feel any connection to God? Does that mean there is no God? In other words, does God's very existence depend on having a personal experience of feeling God's existence?

I believe there is a deeper spiritual knowing that comes as revelation, so that God's existence no longer depends on us saying it is so, or detecting it with our senses. Over time I've come to know that God is everywhere: on a scary car ride with a crazy father, in psychiatric care units, and on death row. You might discover God in places I've never been. That's why I have come to believe that there is nowhere that God is not. God is everywhere.

The Importance of Desert Experiences

It is easy to believe in God when life is overflowing with goodness. We can feel and see God in newborn babies' breath, in dazzling sunsets, in the tender touch of a loved one. But life isn't all warm fuzzies. Life gives us many opportunities to feel pain in God's presence. Sometimes the pain lasts a long time. The Christian tradition is rich with testimony about long periods of suffering. The spiritual experiences of struggling with faith are often referred to as "desert experiences," because the desert represents a place of isolation and scarcity.

In the story of the exodus, after Moses led the people out of slavery in Egypt, they wandered in the desert, lost and afraid. They were angry with Moses and with God, blaming both for their suffering. The people even complained that life in slavery was better than life in the desert. The desert is a place of hard times.

The Bible tells another story about the desert. Jesus often sought deserted places to pray. He encouraged his disciples to get away from the hustle and bustle, to find a place where they could be alone for a time of rest and prayer. But along with the solitude of the desert come trials and temptations. After all, it was in the desert that the devil tempted Jesus. The testimony of scripture reminds us that being united with God, even in times of focused prayer, does not guarantee a painless or easy life.

I've nevertheless found spiritual renewal in times of solitude and prayer in the desert. As a college student, at the urging of my chaplain, I spent a summer volunteering as a Christian minister in a remote corner of the North Rim of the Grand Canyon. Hiking the trails through this rugged landscape, my spirit found a home among all the living things flourishing in the desert. As tourists gathered for Sunday morning worship in the Grand Canyon Lodge, I simply pointed outside to the layers of rock and said, "Look and see! How beautiful is all of creation!" I felt the joy of leading people in praise and prayer, and sensed God's gentle call into ministry. Free from day-to-day distractions, without the familiar faces, without the obstruction of trees or buildings, a visit to the desert forces you to slow down and have a closer look. I have returned to the Grand Canyon twice since that summer. Each time, I am reminded of God's Spirit that moves powerfully to change and transform all of creation. The current climate crisis our planet faces threatens not only our physical well-being as we quickly approach the time when we will have to search for limited resources such as clean water, air, and food. Climate crisis also threatens our spiritual and psychological well-being. One of the greatest challenges ahead is whether or not we will be able to adapt to our new, depleted environment. I imagine that living in an unhealthy planet will only make sustaining mental health even more difficult.

When faithful Christians share with me their stories of personal hardship, distress, crises of faith, and suffering, it often surprises them to learn how many of those struggles they share with spiritual giants Mother Teresa and Mahatma Gandhi. Both religious figures are famous for changing the world through their profound dedication to serving the least of these—people society casts away—the orphans, the poor, the sick, the sinners, the unclean. It is easy to idolize Mother Teresa and Gandhi and to forget their humanity. Now, long after their deaths, stories are coming to light about how both of them struggled with doubt, despair, and depression.

Did Mother Teresa ever question God's existence?

Yes.

Did Gandhi experience depression and hopelessness, enough to attempt suicide?[2]

Yes.

It turns out even God's own beloved son, Jesus, didn't feel God's presence in his own time of great suffering. At the time of his execution, Jesus cried out to God, "My God, my God, why have you forsaken me?"

Being spiritual does not protect us from life's suffering. I once naively thought that being Christian would save me from sadness and protect me from pain. I thought, *If God watches over me, then why would God allow me to suffer?* Likewise, *If Jesus lives in my heart, then how could my heart be sad?*

Faith is not an anti-depressant. It cannot be swallowed in order to rewire our brains for happiness. Rather, faith allows us to accept the coexistence of God and suffering. We do not have to choose between two realities, because, if we did, God would have to go. There is no way we could deny the existence of suffering. I believe God exists in this messed-up world, and, in the moments of greatest pain, God is there to wipe away our tears. After all, we aren't the only ones crying. God is crying too.

What the Mystics Can Teach Us

It is possible for pain to be a gateway to deeper spiritual connection to God? The Christian mystics, through their long tradition, testify to the ways in which periods of what we would today call mental illness were actually times of deepening spiritual development. Religious scholar Ursula King defines a mystic as someone who experiences a burning desire to be united with God.[3]

Looking back in time, we have testimonies from Christian women who wrote about the spiritual life and various experiences of feeling pain in the midst of God's presence. Hadewijch of

Brabant was a thirteenth-century Flemish mystic. She was a spiritual guide to a group of laywomen called Beguines, who lived an ideal of Christian spirituality in self-sufficient communities in different parts of Europe. In Hadewijch's writings she probes the contradictions of the spiritual life and testifies to God's love even in times of pain and suffering. The following excerpt is from the English translation of one of her poems:

> Sometimes burning and sometimes cold,
> Sometimes timid and sometimes bold,
> The whims of love are manifold…
> Sometimes gracious and sometimes cruel,
> Sometimes far and sometimes near…
> Sometimes light and sometimes heavy,
> Sometimes somber, and sometimes bright,
> In free consolation, in stifling anguish,
> In taking and in giving,
> Thus live the spirits
> Who wander here below,
> Along the paths of Love.[4]

Nothing is known of the state of Hadewijch's mental health. There are no medical records to report whether or not she was clinically depressed, but her words describe what happens to us in life as we encounter low periods, lonely periods, times when hope and light seem very far away. I find her honesty refreshing as she gives us permission to acknowledge that a life of faith is not an easy or perfect life, but one filled with varying levels of contentment. This permission to be a sad Christian may seem odd, but I've experienced Christian communities who interpret a lack of joy as a sign of a lack of faith. According to them, the solution to sadness is simple: ask Jesus to make you happy.

If Jesus alone is the answer to our problems with depression, then what does the Bible say about mental health? Looking at stories in the Bible, we encounter a number of people who according to today's definitions of mental illness, show symptoms that could have gotten them "Baker Acted" by the Pharisees.

Delusions are a common symptom of mental illness. There can be a fine line between *delusions* and *visions*—which are manifestations of spiritual enlightenment. Sacred texts tell us of Moses, who hears God's voice bellowing out from a burning bush; Abraham, who hears God's voice instructing him to kill his first-born son; Mary, who hears an angel of the Lord tell her she is going to conceive a child without having sex; and Jesus, who at his own baptism sees God coming to him like a dove from heaven. Seen through the lens of faith, delusions are gifts from God. Yet, from a medical perspective, "spiritual visions" could be a sign of mental illness.

University of Missouri Professor of Psychiatry Armando Favazza says in his book *PsychoBible* that mental health professionals regularly encounter patients with mental illness "who claim to be God or to have a unique relationship with God. They may identify with either an expansive, all powerful God or with the suffering, persecuted Jesus. Such delusions of grandiosity are attempts to reconstruct reality and to provide a meaningful context for their psychopathology."[5] Favazza argues that the medical lens views experiences of religious visions not as manifestations of enlightened spirituality, but symptoms of mental illness.

As a person of deep faith, I am aware of the stigma I carry within me because I have "crazy" in the blood of my family. This stigma associated with mental illness causes emotional stress that negatively impacts well-being. The fear alone of being publicly labeled "crazy" jeopardizes a person's mental health. Because of the mental illness experienced by both my biological father and brother, I often question my own mental health. Even though during my preparations to become an ordained minister I've undergone mandatory thorough psychological evaluations, with healthy results, that doesn't relieve me of the anxiety that crazy is in my blood. Personally, I am hyper alert for any signs of clinical depression or mania. As I've matured in my faith, I've come to understand myself as a mystic. Yet because of the crazy in the blood of my family, this gift of mysticism is often shadowed by my own fear that *mysticism* is actually a code word for *crazy*. Reading about the creative life of artists, writers, and poets, such as author Sue Monk Kidd, has helped me understand that the creative mind sees things that others do not see. I've come to accept my visions as a spiritual gift, and not manifestations of mental illness.

In the months spent preparing to give birth to my son, I learned as much as I could about natural childbirth and discovered a method called hypno-birthing. I was not an early convert to natural childbirth, but chose this alternative after my leaving my first few visits to the doctor's office feeling like I was part of a puppy mill. There were so many women coming and going that our urine specimens lined the shelf in the bathroom. As I explored my options, I was delighted to find a childbirth center near my home. I took their class called Christian Hypno-Birthing, which taught us the technique utilizing mental imagery and prayer as a way to transform pain into pleasure. Midway through my pregnancy, I had a vision in which an old woman said to me, "You have done this before." This vision inspired and encouraged me, affirming that, yes, as a woman, I have done this before. Not because I had, at that time, given birth before, but because a woman's body is designed to give birth and has done so since the beginning of time, billions of times. Yes, I have done this before. At the time of my son's birth, more visions emerged. During my contractions I soaked in a deep warm tub and the hour before he was born, I saw a vision of a mother dolphin and her newborn calf, filled with joy, swimming side by side in the blue ocean. Then at the moment of my son's birth, God filled my body and God's Spirit rushed through me, bringing new life into this world. For that moment I felt at peace and at one with God, consumed by God…in a vision of God's indwelling in human form.

How we choose to interpret people's experiences, whether as spiritual visions or as psychotic delusions, powerfully shapes our understanding of God's presence in the world. It would be heretical to claim that Moses, Abraham, and Mary, and Jesus were delusional and possibly mentally ill. And what of the visions experienced by the many prophets and saints who've emerged since the biblical record? What are we to say of their experiences of spiritual visions? Were they all delusional too?

Fourteenth-century mystic Julian of Norwich experienced sixteen spiritual visions on her deathbed. Julian lived in a cell attached to a church, where she dedicated her life to prayer, contemplation, reading, and writing. At the age of thirty she nearly died from a fever but recovered from her illness to author the first book written in the English language by a woman, *Revelations of Divine Love*. In it, she describes her visions. One recurring theme in Julian's writing is how these visions helped her to accept emotional pain and sorrow as companions within her spiritual life. She testifies:

> This vision was shown to me, as I understand it, because it is helpful for some souls to have such experiences, sometimes to be strengthened, sometimes to falter and be left by themselves. God wishes us to know that he safely protects us in both sorrow and joy equally. And to benefit his soul, a man is sometimes left to himself, though not always because of sin; for at this time the changes were so sudden that I could not have deserved by sinning to be left alone. Neither did I deserve the feeling of bliss. But our Lord gives generously when he so wishes and sometimes allows us sorrow; and both come from the same love. So it is God's will that we should hold on to gladness with all our might, for bliss lasts eternally, and pain passes and shall vanish completely for those who are saved. And therefore it is not God's will that we should be guided by feelings of pain, grieving and mourning over them, but should quickly pass beyond them and remain in eternal joy.[6]

In Julian's vision we hear her testify that suffering, such as with mental illness, does not result from sin. Nor is it a gift from God. Instead, feelings of pain in the presence of God "benefit

[the] soul." We can experience pain in God's presence, and need not question whether or not we are loved or saved.

Life, Even with Illness, Is a Gift

In their book *Inviting the Mystic, Supporting the Prophet: An Introduction to Spiritual Direction,* Katherine Marie Dyckman and L. Patrick Carroll outline the stages of spiritual development, saying that painful life experiences are an important part of faith development. Described as times of deep anguish and meaninglessness, when God feels far away, these experiences of desolation are considered a critical stage of spiritual development. Our experiences of God's absence create within our souls the space to hold God's returning presence.[7]

Faith is waiting in pain for God's presence to be known. When we do not sense God's presence in the midst of our pain, it is "because of our own remoteness, not God's."[8] Searching for God is painful. I've learned I cannot endure this sacred journey alone. Over the years I've collected a community of fellow pilgrims, mentors, and friends who know my vulnerabilities and my fears. To strengthen my own mental health, at various times I've sought out the support of therapists, counselors, pastors, and spiritual directors and, with their help, created safe spaces for me to reflect on my life's journey, to ask the hard questions, and to face difficult truths. I've discovered that physical movement, such as yoga and walking, help me integrate my mental health with my physical and spiritual health. When I have neglected taking care of myself, it's my body that speaks to me the loudest, letting me know through migraine headaches that I've got to get back into balance.

People who live with mental illness, and those who love them, know what it is like to feel intense and unremitting pain. As a chronic brain disease with biochemical roots, mental illness changes over time. Some weeks are better than others. And the cumulative effect of mental illness takes its toll. Over the course of several years, decades even, mental illness alters a person forever. There are also severe side effects from the psychotropic medications often prescribed: weight gain, kidney failure, tremors, slowing of small motor functions, and lethargy. To live with mental illness is to suffer daily. Turning to spiritual practices such as prayer and meditation can help bring comfort and a sense of inner peace during times of suffering.

As I prepared to share my testimony about the experiences with my family and mental illness, I turned to ancient spiritual practices, seeking God's guidance, wisdom, and courage. While on sabbatical I visited the Chartres Cathedral in France and walked its world-famous labyrinth. The Chartres labyrinth is thought to be one of the most powerful spiritual centers in the world, and is on land that is believed to be an ancient site of goddess worship. When I visited the Cathedral's crypt and gazed deep down into the well that is found there, I experienced a vision of God's umbilical cord, connecting this holy place to the womb of God. Then, walking into the heart of the labyrinth, I experienced another vision in which two strangers stood with me in its center. I felt drawn to look into the eyes of the young man and young woman, and it was Jesus and his faithful disciple Mary Magdalene who had entered the labyrinth center with me. Mary's presence with me in the labyrinth confirmed the importance of feminine companions and offered me a model of faithful friendship. Mary traveled with Jesus as one of his followers and refused to leave his side, even at the time of his crucifixion. All four Gospels name Mary as present at Jesus' tomb and the Gospel of John says she is the first witness to the resurrection of Jesus. Mary's relationship with Jesus had to do with her ability to experience and embrace God's revelation in Jesus Christ. Mary was there that day in the labyrinth to encourage me to more fully open myself up to the power of God in Jesus Christ. I locked eyes with Jesus, and he nodded yes and my heart raced. I knew that God would help me understand the crazy in the blood that runs through my family and that Jesus would be with me to help me to tell my story of faith. With God as my midwife, I was to give birth to my own testimony.

If I preach from the pulpit about a vision from God, it is seen as a spiritual gift. But if I post on Facebook a status update about my vision, some will think it's a manifestation of mental illness. How do we know if a vision is a gift from God or a delusion and symptom of a neurological disease? The medical manual for diagnosing mental illness (*Diagnostic and Statistical Manual*, or *DSM*)[9] explains that widely held religious or cultural beliefs and phenomena are exempt from classification as symptomatic of mental illness. So apparently spiritual visions, when validated by a faith community, represent wellness, even giftedness, and not disease. Sharing the spiritual life within a community of faith is an important part of maintaining mental health. It's the difference between standing alone testifying on a street corner and standing in a pulpit testifying to a congregation.

One way that Christians living with mental illness have interpreted their disease is to believe that it is a spiritual gift from God. While I don't agree, I understand how someone could view it that way. Katie is a friend of mine who struggles with bipolar and she says that without her illness, she would not have known how much she needed God. Katie believes that if she were healthy, then she would be more arrogant and less dependent on God. The tricky part about this theology is when we begin to view mental illness as part of God's plan. Does God give otherwise beautiful people mental illness to keep them humble?

I hear church members say, "God never gives you a cross that you cannot bear." Others say, "God doesn't give you more than you can handle." I'm not sure this is helpful, and it's a misquote of scripture. Does God give certain people mental illness because God knows they are strong enough to handle it? How do you then explain suicide? Were they too weak to handle God's gift? From what I have witnessed and experienced in my life, I simply cannot bring myself to accept that mental illness is a spiritual gift from God.

What makes more sense to me is that, through a life of faith and in relationship with God, we can experience life with mental illness as a gift. I believe that God is the giver of life, and life is a gift. That life is filled with diseases that cause us pain and suffering is not God's doing. What I know from having crazy in the blood is this: mental illness is not a gift and it is not a curse. Mental illness is a biochemical reality, like cancer, and heart disease, and all the things we wish would go away. Mental illness is no more a gift from God than cancer.

Experiencing the pain of mental illness as a biological brain disease need not interfere with our spiritual development; it can be part of it. It is not our sinfulness that causes mental illness, nor the sins of our fathers. It is not God's punishment. And it is not God's spiritual gift. Mental illness is a disease, a genetic and biological reality. Despite our modern advances in neurological sciences, even the greatest minds in science still do not fully understand the cause of mental illness. Research continues to show that much of the brain remains a mystery, and there is no cure for severe mental illness, only symptom management through a combination of medications, coupled with behavioral and cognitive therapy. And some forms of severe mental illness cannot really be prevented. Some of us are born with crazy in the blood, with genetic predisposition for mental illness. As people of faith, we can understand our experiences with mental illness as experiences rich with God's presence. Our suffering need not be devoid of a loving and compassionate God.

Mother Teresa says of the spiritual life, "Difficult, yes. It's meant to be difficult. Jesus says: 'If you want to be my disciple, pick up your cross and follow me.' He does not force us. He says, 'if you want.'"[10] It is time for the church to acknowledge the many people who bear the cross of mental illness. To pick up the cross of mental illness and follow Jesus is a radical act of faith. Yet too often Christian communities cause more harm and suffering by suggesting that mental illness is something shameful and somehow a sign of unfaithfulness and even sinfulness.

While meeting for lunch with Brad, a local church pastor, he shared with me that in the past five years, six members of his church had attempted suicide. The biggest frustration, he said, was that, in the aftermath of each attempt, not one of the individuals returned to church. When I asked him to explain the reasons why they didn't come back to church, he said he didn't know. He thought it could be because they were ashamed of their mental illness, afraid of rejection by the congregation, or in one case angry at him for having the person Baker Acted. Brad was frustrated by the lack of community available to these individuals who suffered with mental illness, and he was visibly strained by the emotional toll this took on him as he ministered to people in crisis. Even though this minister was caring and compassionate to the members of his church who struggled with mental illness, they still felt like they couldn't be part of the church during their time of greatest need.

Many faith communities still believe and preach that mental illness is strictly a spiritual disease caused by personal sin and not related to biochemistry. According to this belief system, practiced by some members of the nouthetic counseling movement, the solution is not mental health care by medical professionals, but confession of sin facilitated through the church. Followers of the nouthetic (what is now called biblical counseling) movement believe all treatment should be based solely on the Bible and on Jesus Christ and view psychology and psychiatry as secular and therefore incompatible with and even opposed to Christianity.

Here are some interesting and startling statistics:

A third of Americans – and nearly half of evangelical, fundamentalist, or born-again Christians – believe prayer and Bible study alone can overcome serious mental illness.

Thirty-five percent agree with the statement, "With just Bible study and prayer, ALONE, people with serious mental illness like depression, bipolar disorder, and schizophrenia could overcome mental illness."

Fifty percent of those 18-29 years old say prayer and Bible study could overcome mental illness. That number falls to less than 30 percent for those 55-64.[11]

When the church instructs people who are struggling with severe depression that in order to experience healing they must repent for their sins, it drives people further into despair with no hope for healing. When mental illness is viewed strictly as a spiritual disease and not a brain disease, God is often viewed as the one in charge of administering mental illness as a punishment. Viewing mental illness only as a spiritual disease contributes to the stigma and shame of people who suffer from mental illness. It is tragic that Christian communities, the very communities in which sufferers seek compassion, acceptance, understanding, healing, and love, can be the communities that inflict the most harm.

While in demonizing people with mental illness the Christian tradition has been part of the problem, it also has within it great potential to offer support, healing, and compassion. While at a denominational church conference I attended a workshop about mental illness and the church led by Rev. Alan Johnson. Alan is a retired United Church of Christ minister who started raising awareness about mental health at his church in Boulder, Colorado, back in 2007. Since then he's led bi-weekly spiritual support groups for people with mental illness at his local church, works with a Colorado based Interfaith Network on Mental Illness, and also spearheaded the national United Church of Christ's Mental Health Network. I am inspired by Alan's commitment to building a movement in the faith community that creates safe spaces for people to break the silence about mental illness. I wondered why he dedicated so much of his time and energy to this work. I guessed that his life was impacted in some profound way by mental illness, but I didn't know his story. I hadn't heard his testimony. A reserved and humble person, Alan didn't talk a lot about himself. I asked him why he was so passionate about mental health and he said that his adult son was diagnosed with bipolar as a teen.

Alan's Testimony:

I had no way of knowing what was happening to my son when he disappeared in New York City one night. I knew some of his behavior was unusual, and his antics were what I came to understand as manic. It was not until he returned home early in the morning that I was able to put him in a taxi and take him to a local hospital's psychiatric unit. It was the first major step in my coming to grips as a parent in the world of mental illness. While this is now 24 years ago, I can recall it vividly as if it was yesterday.

Today my son is in his forties and he is thriving in his life, striving in his sport, has a healthy job, is witty and funny, and is sensitive and compassionate. It was when he was in his late teens that he learned that he is bipolar and was abusing substances. Through a sharp and caring psychiatrist, finding the right medications, having a tremendously supporting wife, a loving family, and a strong appreciative group of clients, he shines through. It has been through many hospitalizations and some very bleak times that he and we have come. He has needed to respect the biological conditions which led to the bipolar diagnosis, and he has learned how to live with them. He has managed well. I am very proud of him.

As a parent, many times I just held on with dear life to the roller coaster ride of finding balance in my days. I was constantly attuned to the "feelings" that were communicated in our conversations, ever alert to the "signs" of the manic or even the hypomanic stages of bipolar. Although I did not always ask directly, "how are you doing?"—because I had asked that so many times—it was the question always lurking in the background. At many junctions, I realized that if my son was sick, I was sick, too. If he was doing well, I was doing well. Supportive listening by my wife, my own therapy, my education about mental illness, and my deeply held Christian faith have brought me to a place where I realize that I have done the best that I could and, while I love and cherish my son, he has his life and I have my life. Simple to say, difficult to live.

The mental health ministry in our church came into being as a result of the senior minister asking me to meet with another member of the church whose two children had died by suicide, as had my brother. All three of them had lived with a mental illness, a brain disorder. When I learned many years later that 87% of people who ended their lives had a diagnosable mental illness, I understood it. My education began not only with reading about bipolar and talking with psychiatrists, but also by taking the NAMI (National Alliance on Mental Illness) Family to Family course along with "In Our Own Voice." When my biological family sat down after my brother's death, we all talked about how we would answer people's questions. The five of us had different languages we chose to use: "It is no one's business." Or, "He died by accident." "We don't have to say anything," one said. Finally my dad said, "He died because he was so depressed that the help he received was just not enough. He died by suicide." That was it.

This family experience led me to go deeper into what mental illness is. I wanted to know much more about bipolar and substance abuse. These personal situations drove me to start a mental health ministry in the church in which I was a member. I always knew that the faith community could be a tremendous resource for individuals and families affected by mental illnesses/brain disorders. While we know that one out of four people in our congregations are directly affected by mental illness, very few congregations draw on the Christian story and the community life to provide awareness and support. Bringing the good news of the

gospel to those of us who have experienced hopelessness
and helplessness is a calling of the church. If our faith is
not connected with our life's experiences, even those of us
who have been affected by mental illness, then our faith
is inadequate and truncated. Yet when our Christian faith
is interlaced with our lives, there is a fullness, a richness
and an abundance of love and hope.

Crazy in the blood runs deep in the church, in its clergy, in
its leaders, in its followers, in its saints, and in its sinners. There
needs to be more research and resources to support clergy mental
health. By sharing our testimonies as people of faith, as church
leaders who also experience the pain of mental illness, we witness
to the presence of God in the midst of our suffering. Earlier the
same the night as my brother Scott's most recent suicide attempt,
he confessed to me that he wished there was a spiritual cure
for his disease. He wished that his faith could make him well.
Faith cannot cure mental illness, because mental illness is not
a sin that can be washed away by the blood of Jesus. But faith
can carry the cross and bear the burden of mental illness. Faith
can move us into knowing God's presence in the midst of pain.

Sometimes I wish faith was always a beautiful thing.
But I've come to know that faith sometimes looks ugly and
crazy, just like life itself. In stores across America you can buy
porcelain or jeweled crosses with Bible quotes (though never
the offensive ones) and images of baby bunnies, symbols of
Christian faith for the masses. But what about a cross that
looks crazy, a cross that looks ugly? Not as reflective of a crazy
or ugly God, but one that represents the craziness and ugliness
of our burdens that we bear? I want to see this kind of cross,
because it represents real life too. What would a crazy cross
look like to you?

My story has beauty and ugliness, sanity and craziness. It
is filled with doubt, questions, fear, and death. My testimony
witnesses to growth, rebirth, healing, faith, and God's grace. In
many ways, I am just beginning my journey. My understanding
of God changes over time. The masculine, father images and

language for God no longer speak as strongly to my heart as they once did.[12] These days I connect more to images of God that are beyond male or female form, though the person of Jesus still resonates with my soul. At the time of this writing I am a young clergy woman, thirty-five years old. And I know that the story I have written here is not the final word, but part of a continuing and changing testimony, as time and experience will shape the way I understand what has happened.

In the next chapter I'm going to explore with you how you can tell your story as a testimony of divine love that knows no limits. Healing and wholeness are possible for hearts that have been broken by mental illness. Blessed are the crazy for we will be comforted.

Chapter 6

Blessed Are the Crazy

I hope for healing in this lifetime. I don't want to wait for heaven to experience wholeness. One of the hardest things about severe mental illness is that for most people there is no forever cure, but, instead, a lifelong struggle. I have witnessed firsthand this struggle in the valley of the shadows of depression and death. In my home growing up, in the places where I work, in my family today, people I love suffer from the agony of mental illness. Even under the care of mental health professionals, life is still often difficult for people with mental illness and their families. At times it can seem as if there is no hope and no relief from the suffering.

A young person with severe mental illness kills his mother, twenty children, six teachers, and finally himself. When a horrific tragedy like the December 14, 2012, Newtown, Connecticut, school shooting hits the news cycle, conversations about our nation's mental health care system emerge briefly in the public spotlight. Instead of focusing on the issue of gun control, people with mental illness become the target of our fear. In response to the sensational style of reporting that has caused mental illness, gun ownership, and violent crime to become so tightly interwoven, the United Church of Christ Mental Health Network and the UCC Disabilities Ministries Board have issued the following statement:

> We need to remember that most people with a mental
> illness are **_not_** violent. Most people with a mental illness
> can control their disease with medication and behavior

modification. People who have a mental illness are neither more likely nor less likely to own a gun than other members of our society. They are more likely to be a victim of a violent crime than to commit a violent crime.

As a society we are just beginning to tell our stories in public about mental illness. Getting it out in the open, talking about it on the radio, television, in books, on blogs, in schools, and in churches is progress. The Christian faith endures because there is power in telling truthful stories. Christianity tells the story of a broken but beautiful people and the God who loves them so much that God offers God's own self to give the people wholeness and new life. The church today shares this story with the world because it gives us hope that our brokenness can be healed. Anna Carter Florence says in her book *Preaching as Testimony*, "The distinctive witness of Christianity is that God is manifest in the life and resurrection of Jesus Christ. God shows us and calls us to share the news with others. God shows us and calls us to claim the freedom we would like to be. God calls us to testify."[1]

The power of our testimonies is the power to work through, heal, and eventually transform our suffering. Telling the stories about my crazy father, bipolar brother, executed cousin, and my own spiritual visions makes room for light and air, the things of God's Spirit, to enter in. Keeping these stories as secrets buried deep down in my soul gives them power to hold me captive, isolated by my own fear, shame, and pain: fear that I too, will be labeled crazy and, therefore, unlovable; shame that I am not good enough to be loved; pain because this suffering makes me feel alone in the world. American Poet Laureate Maya Angelou wrote in *I Know Why the Caged Bird Sings* that "there is no greater agony than bearing an untold story inside of you."

Sharing my testimony is liberation. It sets me free from my prison of fear, shame, and pain, and opens the door to new hope, healing, and love. Anna Carter Florence writes that, in the classical sense, testimony is "both a narration of events and a confession of belief: we tell what we have seen and heard, and then confess what we believe about it."[2] I believe that God's story transforms my story as I confess faith in a loving God who walks with me through the shadows of mental illness.

Compassion for Caregivers

Because the stigma attached to mental illness remains so powerful, there is little public recognition of the need to show compassion to people with mental illness, let alone for their caregivers and the family members. Like myself, many people cover up for their family members who have mental illness, making excuses for the member's behavior or telling lies so as to avoid telling the painful truth. Sometimes it is easier to lie than to face the emotionally draining task of explaining to someone the complex issues of a mentally ill loved one. I am tired of lying about just how profoundly mental illness shapes my family's life, because when I cover up the mental illness, then I dig myself deeper into a hole where it gets lonelier and scarier. I distance myself from the company of light and truth.

To tell the true story is to heal. The scientific story continues to unfold, revealing no single environmental, biochemical, cultural, or behavioral cause for any single mental illness, and as more and more people are diagnosed with mental illness, as-yet indecipherable patterns of co-occurring illnesses emerge as well. Today one in four people will experience an episode of mental illness in any given year; one in seventeen people lives with severe, chronic mental illness; and one in ten children and youth experience a mental health disorder (according to nami. org, the website for the National Alliance on Mental Illness). The economic and social costs of untreated mental illness are staggering. Mental health conditions are the second leading cause of workplace absenteeism. Untreated and mistreated mental illness costs the United States $150 billion in lost productivity each year.[3]

Even if medicine can one day cure mental illness, there will still be the need to heal our lives and our society from its ravages. In 1990, former First Lady Rosalynn Carter wrote,

> People with mental problems are our neighbors. They are members of our congregations, members of our families; they are everywhere in this country. If we ignore their

cries for help, we will be continuing to participate in the anguish from which those cries of help come. A problem of this magnitude will not go away. Because it will not go away, and because of our spiritual commitments, we are compelled to take action.

At the 29th Rosalynn Carter Symposium on Mental Health in 2013, it was reported by Kathleen Sebelius, U.S. Secretary of Health and Human Services, that "60 percent of Americans living with a mental health conditions do not receive the care they need… Each year, we lose more than twice as many Americans to suicide as we do to homicide." Sebelius said that the biggest challenge we face around mental health is not in the area of scientific research in search for a cure or better drugs to treat symptoms, but the hardest part is to change people's attitudes about mental illness. She says our biggest challenge "is not a challenge of the head, but of the heart. Just think for a second of how different things would be if everyone felt like they could access treatment without the fear of being judged. Imagine what it would mean if people felt as comfortable saying they were going for counseling as they are for a flu shot or physical therapy."[4] To take action, for people to get the help they need, we need to know what is wrong. It has got to be okay to tell the true story of mental illness. So how can we go about making it okay for people with a mental health disease and their caregivers to speak out? First, we can educate ourselves on some of the basics, to relieve one burden caregivers often carry: that of explaining the technical ins and outs of their loved one's diagnosis. A good place to begin learning more about mental illness is through resources provided by the National Alliance on Mental Illness (NAMI). Operating support groups across the country and providing online resources, NAMI is the world's largest grassroots mental health network.

Bearing Witness in the Church and as the Church

As mental illness becomes more pervasive in our society, people's personal stories have started to emerge. Yet when it comes to the issue of mental illness, the church is slow to embrace its own tradition of testimonies. Instead, the church, perhaps unintentionally, perpetuates the culture of secrecy, shame, and stigma around mental illness. Because of a lack of information or theological beliefs, some faith communities do not understand mental illness.

It is a sin when Christians encourage people with mental illness to stop taking medication and rely only on spiritual remedies such as prayer. Some preachers insist mental illness is only curable through exorcism, explaining that mental illness is a spiritual disease caused by demon possession. The idea that Jesus alone can cure people of mental illness comes from an interpretation of biblical accounts of Jesus healing people. In the gospel of Mark is a story of Jesus healing a man with an "unclean spirit." The man with an unclean spirit lives in the cemetery where he is naked and in chains. He's got crazy in the blood. Jesus bargains with the unclean spirit, granting its request to not be banned from the country, but instead transported from the man to a herd of two thousand pigs. When the unclean spirit enters the pigs, they drown themselves in the sea, committing mass suicide. A clue that the man's "unclean spirit" is mental illness is found in the description of him once he is healed, when he is described as "being in his right mind." We can also interpret this story as one that speaks to the stigma, shame, and isolation that people with mental illness endure. Only when the man is in his right mind is he allowed to be clothed and return to the community. Imagine the healing that is possible when we include people with mental illness, just as they are, as part of our faith communities. This story challenges the way society excludes, isolates, and shames people who suffer from disabilities.

The shame and stigma of mental illness continues on in churches today. I hear too many stories of Christians placing blame on families at a time when the family members are most in need of support, saying, "If only his mother would bring him to youth group, Billy wouldn't be so depressed and anxious." It is a tragedy when faith communities view suicide by a person with mental illness as a sin or an unfaithful act. Then, on top of all the grief involved in the tragic death of a loved one, the family has to deal with the shame and isolation from their community of faith at a time when the family most needs the support of their community.

People with mental illness and their families are often feared, distrusted, and marginalized. Pathways to Promise, an interfaith organization that provides resources about ministry and mental illness (www.pathways2promise.org) reports on their website:

> According to the U.S. Department of Health and Human Services (publication #ADM 86-1407) the two worst things that can happen to a person are leprosy and mental illness. In American society, ex-prisoners stand higher on the ladder of acceptance than people with mental illness. When asked to rank twenty-one categories of disabilities from the least offensive to the most, mental illness was placed at the bottom of the list. Mental illness, unlike other forms of illness, is viewed by society as being socially unacceptable, embarrassing and not to be discussed or acknowledged,"

The complexity and chronic nature of mental illness means that it does not go away easily or quickly. These characteristics of mental illness make it difficult for faith communities to know how to respond in ways that are both meaningful and healing. As Robert Uken, a chaplain at Pine Rest Christian Hospital writes,

> We like to be able to pray and see God at work healing, but when this doesn't happen the way we expect, our own concept of prayer and God is challenged. To rethink, to wrestle with God as well as ourselves is a frightening task. The faith community enters the painful realm of suffering. There is the additional burden of unanswered and unanswerable "why?" How tempting it is to take the easier way of withdrawing or coming up with easy answers. How the faith community deals with persons

with mental illness and their families depends on how well it deals with its own brokenness and the pain of life. Does the faith community give the impression that it is not okay to be less than perfect? When we are uncomfortable with our own humanness, our own faults, our own brokenness, it is easy to feel great discomfort being around other people who reveal some of the same human weaknesses and brokenness. In a sense, our own human vulnerability is mirrored by another person who more visibly evidences human frailty.[5]

Families and communities of faith need to be intentional and proactive about changing this culture of shame, secrecy, and stigma. Testimonies only work when there is a place to testify, a safe space to tell the truth. And healing happens when testimonies are given and received within community.

My brother Scott is not afraid to talk with me about his mental illness. Bipolar impacts Scott differently over the course of his life, and he experiences different manifestations of the illness over time. He swings from having a terrible few months of hell, followed by a period of numb detachment, to being excited about planning a new adventure. One of the ways he copes with his illness is to be in regular psychotherapy. His mental health counselors have encouraged him to speak openly about his illness with his family members. So even though it is difficult for me to hear about the depth of his pain, his sharing with me has strengthened our bond and brought us closer. He has asked for help and invited me to walk beside him as he carries his cross. In our honest conversations we can listen, explore, question, and discover God's presence and healing love. My father and brother, in their heart-wrenching struggles with mental illness, have been my greatest spiritual teachers. Crazy in the blood of my family has brought me closer to understanding the power of God's healing love.

There is good news about the positive role of churches breaking the silence about mental illness. In the spring of 2014 megachurch pastor and Purpose Driven Life author Rick Warren hosted the largest gathering of Christians (three thousand in attendance, with thousands more participating online) for a conference about mental illness. What prompted this breaking of the silence about mental illness? Tragically, it was the suicide of Warren's young adult son that propelled the Warrens to help organize a national movement to educate Christians about mental heath. In another breakthrough event held in July of 2014, which Alan Johnson attended, over 40 leaders gathered in Arlington, Virginia, representing diverse faith, psychiatric and other mental health leaders to inaugurate the Mental Health and Faith Community Partnership, a collaboration between psychiatrists and clergy aimed at fostering dialogue between the two professions, reducing stigma and helping people receive both medical and spiritual care.

Churches can create environments in which it is safe to tell the truth about mental illness by inviting people into small groups to share their own personal testimonies of struggle with mental illness. What Alan has created in his church in Boulder is a model that other churches can follow. In settings like this, people can feel safe enough to freely explore and question what it means to be loved by God while facing mental illness. NAMI has a specific outreach program called NAMI FaithNet that provides an easy-to-use curriculum called "Reaching out to faith communities." Mental Health Ministries (www.mentalhealthministries.net) also has a training guide for congregations that provides educational resources for faith communities to help reduce the stigma of mental illness, and promote inclusion, welcome, and spiritual support for people with mental illness and their families. Together people can find pathways for healing.

According to a University of Missouri Department of Health Psychology study of people across five different religions, increased spirituality does lead to better mental health.[6] Participating in a religious organization breaks us free from isolation by creating community. Within communities of faith we often find support to cope with everyday stress and crises that arise, such as illness, birth of a first child, job loss, financial stress, and death. A life oriented toward faith is directed outward, less focused inward, and satisfies our longing for spiritual oneness. Religion offers us meaning for our complex lives and provides a narrative of comfort and hope. Clergy are often the first responders to mental health crises. People often will first turn to their minister, priest, or other spiritual leader during times of personal or family distress.

Leaders can model the power of telling the truth, acknowledge the manifestations of mental illness in our communities, and create a culture that focuses on ways to bring healing instead of casting judgment. We can call upon our communities of faith to organize around advocacy on public policies regarding mental health care. For the best resource on current public policy issues go to the NAMI Internet Advocacy Action Center (www.nami.org) for legislative alerts and updates, including steps we can take to stop budget cuts to mental health care. As Christians we recall Jesus' way of blessing those who are marginalized: the sick, the hungry, the poor, the imprisoned. Jesus blesses people who have mental illness, extending divine love, grace, and spiritual healing. Blessed are the crazy for we shall be called children of God.

Prayer

No, Jesus cannot wash away the crazy in the blood of mental illness. No, God will not give my brother Scott a new, disease-free brain. But Jesus watches over my brother and creates in him a clean heart. The burden of suffering can be shared so that it's not soul-crushing. And God comforts me as I walk beside loved ones who carry the cross of mental illness. I experience the still-speaking God in the words of hope found in Psalm 23. Inspired by the witness of scripture, I weave my personal testimony today with that of the psalmist from long ago, creating a faithful interpretation of God's love for every generation.

Inspired by Psalm 23

Jesus is my light and gives me all that my spirit needs to carry on. God invites me to trust in divine love so that when the still water runs thick with crazy blood, my soul is restored. God leads me down paths of giving my testimony for the sake of healing. Even though I walk through the valley of the shadow of mental illness with crazy in the blood, I will fear no evil, for God is with me. God's Spirit comforts me. God prepares a table for all who carry the cross of mental illness; God makes sure there's abundance, more than enough of everything for everybody. Surely goodness and mercy will follow me all of the days of my crazy life. And I will be in the blessed presence of God's healing light and love forever.

There are many other scriptures that are helpful in times when we desire healing from our pain. Psalm 139 dares us to trust that God's Spirit is ever-present, even in the hell caused by suffering from mental illness. God will guide us out of the hell of our long and painful nights, holding us, and leading us to the brightness of God's healing daylight. The psalm concludes with the promise that we are all wonderful works of God's creation, knit together in our mother's womb, even those of us with crazy in the blood pulsing through our veins.

Another psalm puts to words common symptoms of depression: sadness, anger, isolation, abandonment, mistrust, spiritual emptiness, and hopelessness. Psalm 88 says, "You have put me in the depths of the Pit, / in the regions dark and deep… / O LORD, why do you cast me off? / Why do you hide your face from me?" (vv. 6, 14, NRSV). It's hard to get angry at a disease. Sometimes blaming God is the closest we can get. By crying out to God in lamentation, we can express honestly how frustrating it is to suffer from chronic, incurable disease. Sometimes having a disability feels like a curse from an angry God.

Ultimately scripture witnesses to a divine love for all of creation that overpowers all that threatens our wellbeing. This love is

what saves us. In Romans 8:38–39, the apostle Paul captures the
nature of this love when he testifies that "neither death, nor life,
nor angels, nor rulers, nor things present, nor things to come, nor
powers, nor height, nor depth, nor anything else in all creation,
will be able to separate us from the love of God in Christ Jesus
our Lord." (NRSV). Nor mental illness, I would add.

It takes courage and strength to speak of the agony, hardship,
and heartache of not only living with mental illness, but also
loving someone with mental illness. Mental illness is cross for
all of us to bear and cannot be carried alone. Scripture says we
are to "bear one another's burdens, and in this way you will
fulfill the law of Christ" (Gal. 6:2, NRSV). Spiritual support
found in communities of faith as well as personal prayer gives
us strength to help one another carry this cross.

People of faith have what Susan Gregg-Schroeder calls a
"spiritual imperative" to help one another bear the burden of
mental illness. Gregg-Schroeder is the founder of Mental Health
Ministries (www.mentalhealthministries.net) and is public about
her own experiences with mental illness. Her life is a testimony to
the transformational power of carrying the cross of mental illness
into the daylight of public ministry as an educator and advocate
for mental health ministries. Her work is inspired by her faith,
and the witness of all the world's religions that teach us to share
one another's burdens and to care for all who suffer. All of God's
people are called to be faithful, to love one another, to reach out
to those who are broken and to seek justice for all God's people.

Yes, I want to believe with all my heart and mind that healing
is possible in this lifetime. Susan Gregg-Schroeder says:

> Healing is the peace that comes from knowing that
> God is working in our lives to bring about the best
> possible outcome, which is healing mind, body and
> spirit. This sense of peace and wholeness are gifts from
> a loving and compassionate God even as we learn to
> live with mental illness. The challenge we face today
> is not the choice between faith and science. We need
> both. Medications may stabilize symptoms. But it is

relationships, connections to others and love that heal the soul.[7]

My high school teacher George Frissell, who also taught the course "Classical Ideas and World Religions" to my sister and three brothers before me, knew about my family. My senior year in high school, when God and love felt very far away, Mr. Frissell walked by me in the hallway after school. He looked into my eyes and asked me what was wrong. My eyes welled up with tears and my body began to shake. I couldn't speak. He walked me to his classroom, sat me down at a desk and handed me tissues. I don't think I ever answered his question that afternoon. He didn't demand an explanation. He was comfortable simply holding the safe space for my pain to untwist itself. He was the first male in my life to show me the healing power of silence and compassion.

Mr. Frissell gave me a book for graduation called *Peace Is Every Step: The Path of Mindfulness in Everyday Life* by Vietnamese Zen master Thich Nhat Hanh. This book explains what Mr. Frissell was doing that afternoon: he was practicing mindfulness and this meant that he took the time to truly see me. In being seen by another, I felt alive.

If Christianity reveals to me the healing light of Christ, then Buddhism teaches me that awareness of the causes of suffering leads to healing. The first step to transforming the suffering caused by mental illness is to pay attention to it. The problem with ignoring mental illness when it is present in yourself or someone you love is that it can take on a destructive life of its own. We can easily become a victim of mental illness instead of a survivor. Being mindful of how mental illness impacts your life leads to empowerment and healing. Practicing mindfulness wakes us up from denial about our realities. If our reality includes mental illness, then practicing mindfulness can open up pathways to healing because it raises our awareness.

The practice of mindfulness is embedded in the Christian scriptures and tradition. Centering prayer is an ancient Christian practice that uses mindfulness techniques that dates back to early monastic traditions and writings of Christian mystics described in the anonymous fourteenth-century classic *The Cloud of Unknowing,* and in the writings of Christian mystics such as John Cassian, Francis de Sales, Teresa of Avila, John of the Cross, Therese of Lisieux, and Thomas Merton. Enjoying popularity in Christianity today is the practice of *Lectio Divina* (means "divine reading" in Latin), which is an ancient monastic practice of reading scripture with periods of silence interwoven with repeated readings of the same scripture in order to help us let go of our own agenda and to be open to what God might be saying to us.

The purpose of Christian mindfulness is to open our hearts and minds to the still-speaking God, to create time and space for the indwelling of Christ's Spirit among us. When we are living with mental illness, it is important to embrace our identity as children of God and receive into our weary spirits God's abundant blessings.

Mental illness cannot be wished or prayed away. The stigma and shame about mental illness only increases its destructive power. Hiding in our closets, we are swallowed up in its shadows. It is my confession that by exposing mental illness to the healing light of God, through testimony, through carrying one another's burdens, through therapeutic circles of care, we can find hope and strength. It is my hope that the church can be a community of truth tellers, decreasing stigma as we create safe, welcoming spaces for people with mental illness. It is my testimony that the God of love is with us, even when there's crazy in the blood. It is my gospel truth that blessed, not cursed, are the crazy for we will be called children of God.

Epilogue

On May 23, 2014, underneath a red sun, I officiated my brother's wedding. It was Steve's second marriage, and all five of us siblings with crazy in the blood were there to witness the beginning of another chapter being written in our family. My brothers Scott and Stuart stood next to Steve as he promised to love until death, the brothers clad in khaki pants, white Mexican wedding shirts, and brown flip flops from Wal-Mart. At the wedding reception we celebrated as Jesus would have us do: wine flowing, hips swaying, and children armed with sparklers leaping in the starry night.

For this moment, the intensity of past encounters with the insanity of our father, our cousin's painful death, and our brother's struggle for mental health, reminds us that the crazy in our blood will always be a part of us, even during times of joy and celebration. Over the past year Scott's mental health has improved significantly as a result of his sobriety (not mixing pills with alcohol), a new medication that has eliminated his thoughts of suicide, his active participation in a 12-Step program, and his community volunteering at the local men's jail. Scott continues to see a psychiatrist and a psychologist as part of his support system. In the past year Scott has taken in a roommate who is a single dad with a three-year-old child, for whom Scott's been a second father, and he's done an amazing job with the boy. I am proud of my brother. For a while Scott asked me to assist him by providing financial oversight to help him monitor his spending. When he no longer wanted to die, he wanted to live for the first time. So he went on some spending binges that he later regretted, such as a cross-country trip to California on his motorcycle and giving money away to people who asked for his help. He's told me about a few people he regularly gave money to and how guilty he felt about refusing their requests. I believe that people are preying upon his vulnerability and targeting him for easy money.

My brother's self-esteem has suffered greatly from his mental illness and so this lack of confidence makes him feel like he has to buy his friendships, especially female companionship. The stigma and shame of having a brain disorder is part of the cross Scott carries. According to Mental Health First Aid, "Stigma is a cluster of negative attitudes and beliefs that motivate the public to fear, reject, avoid, and discriminate against people with mental illnesses. Stigma is one of the biggest barriers to recovery. Fighting the stigma and shame associated with mental illness is often more difficult that battling the illness itself."[1] Not long after Steve's wedding, Scott mentioned that his medications are not working as well as they used to and that he's worried he sliding back into a deeper depression. He's upset that his ex-wife ignores his attempts to communicate with her again. At the same time, he's planning a solo motorcycle trip from Florida to Canada, including a spin through the Big Apple on his way to Niagara Falls. My mom and I feel torn about his plans for a grand adventure up the East Coast. Part of me wants him to feel free and to live to the fullest, cruising with crazy in the blood through Times Square without a care in the world. And part of me wants to get him signed up ASAP for outpatient treatment at the Brain Disorders section of the Mayo Clinic in Rochester, Minnesota. The biggest reason he's not getting all of the help he needs is he feels he can't afford the high cost of quality mental health care.

I cannot pretend to know what if feels like to live with a profound disability, living under constant treatment for a severe brain disease, feeling like life keeps getting interrupted by illness. But I can tell you what it's like to love somebody like that: it's deeply disturbing and painfully beautiful, like the cross.

Scott's wish is for mental illness to be viewed like any other major life-threatening disease, such as heart disease or cancer.

He longs for a day when he, like cancer survivors, can have pride in his identity as a person who is a survivor of a brain disease. It would look something like this: a stream of people wearing matching green T-shirts (green is the color for mental health) in a parade, mental health consumers with pride. My brother taught me to use the word *consumer* when referring to a person who is getting mental healthcare because *consumer* is a nonjudgmental word with less stigma. He envisions a world where there is no shame or stigma in having a mental illness.

I asked Scott if there was anything else he wanted readers to know about him. This is what he said.

Scott's testimony:

Recently my AC1 blood tests revealed I have type 2 diabetes, and my doctor has prescribed medicine to help control it. I did not have to be hospitalized for a diabetic coma in order to figure out that I needed treatment. With treatment my blood sugar disease can be mitigated but never cured. There is no blood test for bipolar disorder. I had to be hospitalized when I was 18 for thoughts of self-harm and delusions before the psychiatrists could provide my diagnosis. I remember in the deepest psychosis I wanted to follow the motto to "First do no harm." I resisted treatment for years. I was lucky that my case was rather textbook so that my diagnosis was accurate and my treatment began when I was ready to accept it. With treatment my brain chemistry disease can be mitigated but never cured.

Just as I have to accept certain dietary restrictions for diabetes, I have to accept certain life restrictions for my bipolar disorder. I cannot do drugs or drink alcohol. I have to guard my sleep cycle. I need to maintain a low level of frustration and stress. I cannot deliver the "MESSAGE" that I was sent here to give to the undoctrinated. I need to avoid excess anger and fear.

I am learning to live within my limitations, and to live fully. This is the essence of recovery from mental illness and it is an individual journey one takes with the help of medicine, counseling, support groups, friends and family.

I still fantasize about taking my own life, but my sister the doctor reverend told me that I was a core part of the spirit of my family and I do not want to destroy that. Her love, as well as that of the people I have met who travel the road of recovery, has helped bring me back to a fuller spirit life.

I would love to hear your personal story, so please feel free to connect with me through my blog, www.sarahgriffithlund.com, on my Facebook page at Sarah Griffith Lund, and follow me on Twitter @revlund, or email me at sarahgriffithlund@gmail.com and let me know about your crazy in the blood stories.

Afterword

I sat with my daughter, reading the last installment of Lemony Snicket's *Series of Unfortunate Events*. We had been caught up in Snicket's world for months, savoring every word of disaster and devastation that enveloped the fictional orphans. When the final volume came out, we traveled to New York City so we could buy books that had been signed by the author and the artist.

When we opened the pages, we read how an extraordinary tree grew on a desert island. It was an apple-horseradish hybrid. The children, who had been (as the series title promised) the subject of many horrific incidents, found shelter in the tree.

I looked down at my tiny daughter as we read. I hoped that the image would stay with her and that she would learn to appreciate the powerful metaphor through her life. The tree reminded me of the Seder dinners that I experienced when I was a child. I took the "bitter herb," and the fumes of horseradish bit me, making my eyes water. I didn't think I would find any relief, until we were invited to take the next mouthful. Then that pungent root was replaced by the sweetness of apples. Having the two tastes harkened to the bitterness and sweetness of life.

That particular mixture came back to me when I met Rev. Dr. Sarah Griffith Lund. We had mutual friends, so I was looking forward to having lunch with her. As we greeted one another, her beauty and kindness stunned me.

Now, I hesitate to write that. I am a feminist and I don't believe that a woman should be solely defined by what she looks like. But now that you have read her words and spent time with her testimony, I think it's fair to say. But if you refrained from judging me concerning my pointing out her beauty, then you can judge me now. As a confession, I regret to admit that I assumed that with Sarah's loveliness came a charmed life.

I figured we wouldn't be friends, because she was too nice. When Sarah smiled, tilted her head, and lilted her voice, I figured we had nothing in common. I assumed she was too far removed from the muck of life, as if she had skipped through a field of Astroturf and plastic daisies, and never had the dirt of the everyday touch her.

Of course, it took less than five minutes after we sat down for our meal when I learned how wrong I was. Sarah was sweet, but it was a determined sweetness that was harvested through wisdom. It was as if she had learned to create her own apple-horseradish hybrid. Sarah's kindness came from sucking on that bitter root and demanding the fruit goodness.

One of the most difficult things that we struggle with as pastors and theologians is why bad things happen to good people. As we read Sarah's story, and our hearts break with the pattern on her little dress, we do not come any closer to answering that big "why." Instead we are faced with another realization of our bitter lives. But Sarah's gift to us is not that she answers all the questions. It is that she tells us the truth. She writes about the stories we are told to hide. She opens up the closets and shows us all the skeletons. Not as an exhibitionist, but as someone who has fully tasted that bitter root and understands the healing that comes from telling those secrets we were supposed to keep muffled.

Then Sarah models to us how to demand mercy in the midst of it. Through her work, Sarah shows us how to tell the truth, how that truth can propel us to love our enemies, and how that act can transform our lives.

Carol Howard Merritt

Appendix

Ten steps for Developing a Mental Health Ministry in Your Congregation

These steps are not necessarily sequential. One of the steps may happen before or after other steps in this list. Follow the synergy in your congregation and the context of your congregation may reveal which step may follow another.[1]

1. **Make a commitment** — Before you begin, do some soul searching. Starting a Mental Health Ministry may take considerable time. You need to decide if you are ready to take on a long-term project. It will probably involve disclosing why you are passionate about mental health. Make sure you and your family members are ready to "come out" to your congregation. (It may take but two people in your congregation who have a "calling" to pursue this ministry.)

2. **Educate yourself** — Learn about mental illness. You probably already have "in the trenches" experience with mental illness, which will help you be understanding and compassionate with others. However, if you have not already done so, we recommend you take the NAMI "Family-to-Family" class if you are a family member or the NAMI Peer-to-Peer program if you are a consumer (a person with mental illness). You do not have to be an expert in mental illness to start a Mental Health Ministry, but it is helpful to have a basic understanding of the problems people are likely to face when they are dealing with various diagnoses.

3. **Get buy-in from your clergy/board of directors**/or the congregation itself — The lines of communication and the decision-making chain are different in every congregation. If it is appropriate in your congregation, explain to your clergy and/or board of directors what you want to accomplish and

ask for their support. You may need to educate them. It may take a while for them to grasp the importance of your mission, but don't give up. It may be important to clarify the interface between the pastoral care dimension of your congregation's staff and the work of the Mental Health Ministry.

4. **Form a task force or ministry team** — Get the word out that you are creating a task force or ministry team on mental illness. Set a time and place for the first meeting and announce it in the weekly bulletin, in the monthly newsletter, on the bulletin board, and other appropriate places. You may also extend personal invitations to some people. If appropriate, tell your story or your family's story. Make sure you advertise the meeting far enough in advance that people can save the date. Invite people to show up to help you figure out a plan. Consider making your first meeting a potluck meal after your service.

5. **Decide with your team what you want to offer/accomplish** — Define who you want to serve and how you will go about it. Do you want to offer a support group? If so, will it be for consumers, family members, or both? Do you want (and do you have the skills) to offer support for those who are in the midst of crises, or will you refer those people elsewhere? Will you offer education? If so, what form will that take? Classes? Workshops? Do you want to create a resource center or library? Are your services just for your congregation, or do you want to reach a wider community? Exactly what do you plan to include in the scope of your ministry? Will you cover just the major mental illnesses, or do you want to include other brain differences, such as addictions, brain injuries, dementia, autism, etc.? After you have clarified what you want to do, write a concise mission statement, set some goals, and begin developing strategies to achieve the goals. It is important to have regular meetings. You may meet monthly or bimonthly to review the recent events or programs, to envision the next steps to be taken, and to share new resources available.

6. **Define strategies for keeping the congregation, board, and clergy involved** — Share your mission and goals with your congregation, your board, and your clergy, and ask for each group's blessing. Ask each group to help you be successful. You

might ask the congregation to support you by attending your programs and classes. You might ask the clergy to support you by asking for healing for those with mental illnesses when they pray during services or talking about mental illness in their sermons. You might focus a weekend or a whole worship service on the concerns of mental health, especially during Mental Health Month (May) and/or Mental Health Awareness Week (in October.) You might ask the board to support you by allocating a small budget for your team's use (for speakers, refreshments, handouts, etc.)

7. **Make an inventory of available resources** — Poll the members of your team and find out who they know who might be willing to speak at one of your programs. Talk to the therapists and psychiatrists in your congregation to see who will help. Ask your local NAMI affiliate for a list of resources they offer and leverage them. For example, your NAMI affiliate might offer support groups and classes you could refer people to, or they may be willing to train you to lead your own support group. Check out the resources available at NAMI FaithNET (www.nami.org/namifaithnet) and Mental Health Ministries (www.MentalHealthMinistries.net). Consider creating a resource notebook that members of your congregation can borrow.

8. **Join with other organizations** — Find out which congregations in your area have Mental Health Ministries and meet with them to share ideas. Consider creating an interfaith network on mental illness in your community. Meet with a representative of your local mental health center and let them know what you are doing. Network with other organizations that have similar goals.

9. **Communicate** — It is important that you continue to communicate about your Mental Health Ministry on an ongoing basis. Consider writing articles for your congregation's newsletters on the topics you offer in your classes/forums. Take notes at your classes/forums and post them on your congregation's website so people who didn't attend can still glean some insights. Announce your events in the church bulletin and even the local weekend edition of your newspaper if they are open to the public. Alert you local NAMI affiliate about your events and ask them to help you get the word out.

10. Be prepared to nurture your ministry — Creating a successful Mental Health Ministry takes more than passion. It also takes persistence. Don't get discouraged if you don't immediately see the results you had hoped for. Keep putting one foot in front of the other and you will succeed.

Mental Health and Faith Resources

Websites

- Chicago Catholic Archdiocese, Commission on Mental Illness and Faith and Fellowship for People with Mental Illness, miministry.org.
- Depression and Bipolar Support Alliance, dbsalliance.org. Information on depression and bipolar and listings of consumer support groups across the USA.
- Interfaith Network on Mental Illness(INMI) (www.inmi.us). Resources for clergy, staff, lay leaders and members of faith communities to help effectively develop and nurture supportive environments for persons dealing with mental illnesses and their families and friends. Caring Clergy Project, (www.caringclergyproject.org), a part of INMI, has a series of You Tube videos for clergy on such topics as, "Making a Referral," and a series on suicide.
- Mental Health First Aid, www.mentalheathfirstaid.org. National in-person training program that teaches you how to help people developing a mental illness or in a crisis.
- Mental Health Ministries, mentalhealthministries.net. An interfaith web-based ministry to provide educational resources to help erase the stigma of mental illness in our faith communities. MHM helps faith communities be caring congregations for people living with a mental illness and those who love and care for them, based on the "Caring Congregations" five-step model of education, commitment, welcome, support and advocacy.
- Mental Health Recovery: Wellness Recovery Action Plan, mentalhealthrecovery.com. Focuses on prevention and recovery based on personal responsibility, self-help techniques and community support.
- Mental Illness Education Project, miepvideos.org.

- National Alliance on Mental Illness (NAMI) Faithnet: NAMI FaithNet is a network of NAMI members and friends dedicated to promoting caring faith communities and promoting the role of faith in recovery for individuals and families affected by mental illness. See nami.org/FaithNet.
- National Institute of Mental Health, nimh.nih.gov.
- National Suicide Prevention Lifeline, 1-800-273-TALK (8255) is a 24-hour, toll-free, confidential suicide prevention hotline available to anyone in suicidal crisis or emotional distress, suicidepreventionlifeline.org.
- Pathways to Promise, pathways2promise.org. Includes booklets: *An Introduction to Mental Health Ministry, The Way of Companionship, Organizing a Congregational Mental Health Team,* and *A Toolkit for Mental Health Ministry.*
- United Church of Christ Mental Health Network, mhn-ucc. blogspot.com. Includes toolkits on mental health, liturgical resources for Mental Health Sunday, along with "A Checklist for a Congregation," "The Welcoming, Inclusive, Supportive and Engaged (WISE) Congregation for Mental Health Covenant," and "Developing a Spiritual Support Group for Mental Health and Wellness."

Books

- *An Unquiet Mind: A Memoir of Moods and Madness* by Kay Redfield Jamison
- *Crazy: A Father's Search Through America's Mental Health Madness* by Pete Early
- *Jesus the Village Psychiatrist* by Donald Capps
- *A Pelican of the Wilderness: Depression, Psalms, Ministry, and Movies* by Robert Griggs
- *Spiritually Integrated Psychotherapy* by Kenneth I. Pargament
- *Souls in the Hands of a Tender God* by Craig Rennebohm and David Paul
- *Troubled Minds* by Amy Simpson
- *Wrestling with your Inner Angels: Faith, Mental Illness and the Journey to Wholeness* by Nancy Kehoe
- *Beyond Blue: Surviving Depression & Anxiety and Making the Most of Bad Genes* by Therese Johnson Borchard

Notes

Foreword

1. See Donald Capps, *The Depleted Self: Sin in a Narcissistic Age* (Minneapolis: Fortress Press, 1993).

2. Donald Capps, "Foreword," in Stewart D. Govig, *In the Shadow of Our Steeples: Pastoral Presence for Families Coping with Mental Illness* (New York: The Haworth Pastoral Press, 1999), x–xi. Govig tells the story of his son's mental illness and its effects on the family in *Souls Are Made of Endurance: Surviving Mental Illness in the Family* (Louisville: Westminster John Knox Press, 1994). I have also written about John Govig in *Fragile Connections: Memoirs of Mental Illness for Pastoral Care Professionals* (St. Louis: Chalice Press, 2005), 153–200.

3. In *Stranger in Our Midst: The Church and People with Mental Illness* (St. Paul: Seraphim Communications video).

4. I suggest in *Jesus: The Village Psychiatrist* (Louisville: Westminster John Knox Press, 2008) that several of the healing stories in the gospels suggest that the persons Jesus healed were suffering from mental illnesses, that, in the psychiatric nomenclature of our day, they manifested the symptoms of somatoform disorders.

5. See my *Understanding Psychosis: Issues and Challenges for Sufferers, Families, and Friends* (Lanham, Md. : Rowman & Littlefield, 2010), chap. 5.

6. William Stafford, *The Way It Is: New & Selected Poems* (St. Paul: Graywolf Press, 1998), 52.

Chapter 2: Entrusting My Father

1. Jeffrey Eugenides, *Middlesex* (New York: Farrar, Strous & Giroux, 2010), 352.

Chapter 3: Caring for My Brother

1. C.S. Lewis, *Letters to Malcolm Chiefly on Prayer: Reflections on the Intimate Dialogue Between Man and God* (New York: Harcourt, Brace and World, 1964).

Chapter 4: Holy Spirit on Death Row

1. See Mark Taylor, *The Executed God: The Way of the Cross in Lockdown America* (Minneapolis: Fortress Press, 2001).

2. See Rita Nakashima Brock and Rebecca Ann Parker, *Proverbs of Ashes: Violence, Redemptive Suffering, and the Search for What Saves Us* (Boston: Beacon Press, 2001).

Chapter 5: Feeling Pain in God's Presence

1. Leonard Cohen, "Anthem," on *Live in London*, produced by Steven Berkowitz and Edward Sanders, Columbia, 2009.

2. Nassir Ghaemi, "Depression in Command," *Wall Street Journal* (July 30, 2011).

3. Ursula King, *Christian Mystics: Their Lives and Legacies throughout the Ages* (Mahwah, N.J.: Hidden Springs, 2001).

4. Ibid., 100.

5. Armando Favazza, *PsychoBible: Behavior, Religion and the Holy Book* (Charlottesvile, W.V.: Pitchstone, 2004), PAGE?.

6. Julian of Norwich, *Revelations of Divine Love,* trans. Elizabeth Spearing (London: Penguin Classics, 1998), 64.

7. Katherine Marie Dyckman and L. Patrick Carroll, *Inviting the Mystic, Supporting the Prophet: An Introduction to Spiritual Direction* (Mahwah, N.J.: Paulist Press, 1981).

8. Ibid., 63.

9. *Diagnostic and Statistical Manual of Mental Disorders,* 5th ed. (Arlington, Va.: American Psychiatric Association, 2013).

10. Quoted in Angelo Devananda, *Mother Teresa, Contemplative in the Heart of the World* (Ann Arbor, Mich., 1985), 84.

11. Lifeway Research results cited in Ed Stetzer, "Mental Illness and the Christian: Scripture and Science," *Christianity Today* (June 3, 2014).

12. See Elizabeth Johnson, *She Who Is: The Mystery of god in Feminist Theological Discourse* (New York: Crossroad, 1992) and Rosemary Radford Ruether, *Sexism and God-talk: Toward a Feminist Theology* (Boston: Beacon Press, 1983).

Chapter 6: Blessed Are the Crazy

1. Anna Carter Florence, *Preaching as Testimony* (Louisville: Westminster John Knox Press, 2007), 64.

2. Ibid., xiii.

3. Statistics from mentalhealthminstries.net.

4. Sebelius's speech is available at hhs.gov.

5. From pathways2promise.org.

6. Brick Johnstone et al., "Relationships among spirituality, religious practices, personality factors, and health for five different faith traditions," *Journal of Religion and Health* 51, no. 4 (December 2012):1017–41.

7. From www.mentalhealthministries.net.

Epilogue

1. From mentalhealthfirstaid.org.

Appendix

1. Developed by Joanne Kelly and Alan Johnson with the Interfaith Network on Mental Illness.

Acknowledgments

To the congregation in New Smyrna Beach for the gift of sabbatical time to begin writing.

To Rick Frost, Raymond Judd, Murrell Wilson, Don Schutt, Jim Gertmenian, and Kent Siladi, who all saw in me early on gifts for ministry.

To the congregations that encouraged me to grow in God's love: Shepherd of the Hills, Broadway Christian, All Souls, and Plymouth Congregational Church.

To the Lilly Foundation's Transition into Ministry programs that nurtured my first years of ordained ministry

To Alan Johnson and the United Church of Christ Mental Health Ministry Network

To my Minnesota mom

To Susan Hord Herman for your initial reading of my manuscript and your contribution to this work.

To The Young Clergy Women Project for saying yes.

To my early readers and cheerleaders: Brenda Lovick, Kelsey Grissom, and Alex Hendrickson.

To Shawna Everett for the amazing cover art and design.

To Brad Lyons, Steve Knight, Gail Stobaugh, K.J. Reynolds at Chalice Press for believing in this book

To Donald Capps for breaking the silence and talking about mental illness with seminary students.

To Carol Howard Merritt for encouraging me to write.

To Kim Gage Ryan for her spiritual guidance and support.

To all my siblings Susan, Scott, Steve, and Stuart who know what its like to have crazy in the blood.

To Scott for being you: honest and blessed.

To my mother and best friend Gigi for encouraging me to write a book about our family. Your love is divine.

To my husband Jonathan and our son Carter: families are forever.